THE OLD LIFE

Poetry by Donald Hall

Exiles and Marriages (1955)

The Dark Houses (1958)

A Roof of Tiger Lilies (1964)

The Alligator Bride (1969)

The Yellow Room (1971)

The Town of Hill (1975)

Kicking the Leaves (1978)

The Happy Man (1986)

The One Day (1988)

Old and New Poems (1990)

The Museum of Clear Ideas (1993)

THE OLD LIFE

Donald Hall

For Danielle
& for new life too!
Donald Hall
4/7/01

Houghton Mifflin Company

Boston New York

Copyright © 1996 by Donald Hall

For information about permission to reproduce selections from
this book, write to Permissions, Houghton Mifflin Company,
215 Park Avenue South, New York, New York 10003.

For information about this and other Houghton Mifflin trade and
reference books and multimedia products, visit The Bookstore at
Houghton Mifflin on the World Wide Web at
http://www.hmco.com/trade/.

Library of Congress Cataloging-in-Publication Data

Hall, Donald, date.
The old life / Donald Hall.
p.   cm.
ISBN 0-395-78841-2
I. Title.
PS3515.A3152044   1996
811'.54 — dc20   96-1853   CIP

Book design by Anne Chalmers

Printed in the United States of America

QUM 10 9 8 7 6 5 4 3 2

Many portions of the four poems in this book have been published in the following
magazines, whose editors have kindly granted permission for their inclusion herein:
    "The Night of the Day" and "The Thirteenth Inning" (previously "The Daugh-
ters of Edward D. Boit") first appeared in *Gettysburg Review.*
    Portions of "The Old Life," under separate titles, first appeared in *Agenda, Agni
Review, American Poetry Review, Atlantic Monthly, Best American Poetry, Boulevard,
Café Review, Englymion, Erato, Gettysburg Review, Granite, Green Mountain Review,
Harvard Magazine, Iowa Review, London Review, The Nation, New Criterion, New
England Review, The New Yorker, New York Times, Ontario Review, ONTHEBUS, Par-
tisan Review, Poetry, Poetry Nation, Princeton Library Chronicle, Red Brick Review,
Sewanee Review, Solo, Southern Humanities Review, Southwest Review, Sycamore Re-
view, Tendril, Times Literary Supplement, Threepenny Review.*
    "Without" first appeared in *Poetry.*

IN MEMORY OF

JANE

Contents

❖

THE

NIGHT

OF

THE

DAY

❖

Cool October, Monday night. I waited for kickoff
at nine o'clock as the long day declined
when I turned older than my dark-haired father
ever got to be. I leaned back sleepy in my chair
as the Dallas Cowboys kicker approached the tee
and was startled to hear a pickup in the drive.
At the door I found Larry Lamorte, agitated
and pointing backward down dark Route 4.
"Dawn!" he shouted. "Dawn! There's something
in the road! Heifers! Bulls!"
                                      Looking past him
into the moonless night, I saw bulky forms
that moved heavily on blacktop, as incongruous
as battleships on Eagle Pond. Larry's old Datsun
shuddered as he apologized, "Sorry not to help.
I promised Earlene I'd watch that show about apes."
        I stared through the dark at the creatures:
heifers? Bulls were unlikely. Through the dark
I watched their ruminant motion, black on black,
and thought: If a late night Plymouth hurried
over the hill at sixty-five, somebody could die.
Inside I woke Jane to telephone Peg Smith,
our constable who usually rounded up black Labs,

not Holsteins, and to wake our neighbors
downstreet. After I walked back out, approaching
cow shapes that hovered over macadam, I heard
Dave Perkins's door slam and watched father and son
walk toward me, black moving against blackness,
and heard David hallo through the silence,
"Whose heifers do they be?"

                                When David and I
were boys — and I visited for the summer, up
from Connecticut — all the old Route 4 farmers
kept a few cattle, raised one or two heifers,
and sitting on stools alongside runty Holsteins
squeezed out two cans of bluish milk a day;
the milk truck stopped at dawn. In return
for the old men's haying, milking morning and night,
hauling ice from the pond for summer's milk,
and raising field corn, H. P. Hood & Co.
mailed them a monthly check, sometimes as much
as twenty dollars. The summer I was thirteen,
my grandfather and I spent an August day chasing
two wild heifers that escaped from a pasture,
but tonight's skinny creatures were tame. Whose
could they be? Nobody raised cattle nowadays
in this valley of old pastures becoming woodlots
(houselots sometimes, and sometimes video
outlets) with only a few fields flat enough
for a tractor to work in; now, to break even,
you needed to milk fifty registered pedigreed
Holsteins — and borrow from Fleet to buy
a milking machine, a stainless-steel cooling tank,
a Macintosh computer, and a frontloader
to spread manure on three hundred hayable acres —

and still you worked sixteen hours;
or you labored all week at the mill to support
your addiction to Holsteins.
                              David and Paul and I
cowboyed the seven heifers from Route 4
to the field beside our barn where their ancestors
had chomped for a hundred years. Whose could
they be? I called my cousin Sherman Buzzle
— selectman, deer hunter, carpenter, pig raiser;
who knew every voter in Wilmot by name —
and woke him where he lived two miles away
in a white Cape with many sheds that our common
great-grandfather built, and asked him
if anybody nearby still kept a herd of cattle.
Sherman was curious. Right after I hung up
(Jane bundled herself into three sweaters
and came outside to help), Sherm's 4 x 4 GMC
maneuvered into the driveway, and he swaggered
to join us — forty years old, hitching green
workpants under his belly, burly or maybe fat
but strong — and peered through darkness
at loose heifers munching asters by the barn.
    Then Peg Smith's new Ford braked at the margin
of the road with her flashers flashing,
and she heaved uphill to join us. Just behind,
her deputy Ned Buttrey parked his Plymouth van,
sparking another cadence, and approached
grinning with one tooth. Ned looked back
at Route 4's shoulder blinking on-and-off,
said, "Looks like quite some party," and laughed,
joining our circle.
                    We gossiped together,

mostly ignoring the heifers that mostly
ignored us back as they moseyed to browse.
Now I saw the cattle clearly enough: young,
not yet bulked-out, bony, old-style Holsteins.
Somebody driving down Route 4 saw car lights
pulsing; he braked, backed up, parked, turned
his flashers on, and joined us. Now we were eight,
but David said goodnight; he needed to load
his truck at five; and Paul went to high school,
David reminded us, who had left school at fourteen.
The quiet father and son walked home together.
I noticed how, not thinking of anybody watching,
they were holding hands.
                              Sherman listed neighbors
who kept cows: Bill Marcik across the pond,
who raised sheep for the wool that his wife Sally
spun and wove, kept a few decorator Holsteins;
but *seven* heifers? We agreed it couldn't be Bill.
Jane mentioned Willy DeLord; when she said his name,
everyone laughed. Sherman spoke common knowledge:
"Willy likes to fence the front of his pasture.
He never gets around to fence the back."
But Willy's disheveled hill farm straggled
on Ragged Mountain five miles north, too far
for Willy's heifers to wander. Peg had a thought:
"Maybe perhaps Ed Ek keeps cows?" Knowingly
Sherman nodded. "Penelope," he said. "But Penny
died on Ed last year November. Old age."
Ned remarked that Sherm remembered names of cows
even though they never voted, "or hardly ever."
We laughed and stomped our feet. The stranger

6

said maybe these cows were wild, like the bears
that came back to our woods after a hundred years.
I told him I liked the notion of feral cows
returning to this New Hampshire valley
of disappearances.

                Then I went back inside
to telephone Bill Marcik, just to *do* something,
and Bill answered, "Well, let me see.
Mother and daughter were there at eight o'clock.
Want me go see? I'll take a look." I told him no;
I doubted even *his* two cattle could multiply
into seven so fast. "Do you have an idea
whose they might be?"

                "Try Willy," Bill said.
Walking back, I heard the sound of stories
in a laugh that rose abruptly from the circle,
from pale faces over sweaters and down jackets
beside the barn — a laugh that ended a story
with gaiety's flare, like a wooden match striking
gold inside a stove. I said, "They're not Bill's.
Bill said try Willy." Nobody had an idea;
nobody fretted. Somebody started to tell the one
about the bull butting the vet that brought syringes.

    Well, *I* fretted: "What do I *do* with them?"
Sherm offered: "Feed them poems. They tell
you've got extra. They tell you keep old bales
of poems stacked in the hayloft."

                We kept a roof
over our tie-up, but no cows stirred under shingle
since my grandfather's heart gave out
thirty years ago. Did I want to wear overalls?

The Night of the Day

For a moment I milked the cattle of daydream
morning and night; but no: I knew how I wanted
to spend my day. I farmed in the summers of boyhood
and that was enough of farming.

But whose heifers
were they? I jogged inside to ring up
Willy DeLord, asleep five miles away or not.
When I told him who I was, and said I was sorry
to wake him, and mentioned the heifers,
Willy's doleful voice ascended to interrupt me:
"Ohhh, *darn*. Ohhh, *darn*. I'll be down — *darn!*
darn! — as soon as I find my pants."

With Willy
on his way, Jane and I alone could have kept
the heifers in place, but nobody wanted
this impromptu party to end; we felt giddy,
the way children do when something extraordinary
keeps them up past bedtime and rules are broken,
all rules are broken, as they are in Paradise.
Sherm told about plowing one February morning
at three o'clock as a snowstorm finished:
"I was scraping Jones's driveway up near Willy's
and saw the electric light in Willy's tie-up."
He found Willy sound asleep, snoring, his head
rising and falling on a Holstein's ribcage.
I remembered my grandfather's tales of Pete Butts,
the Willy DeLord of another day. Peter Butts
planted corn in August and stacked hay in his barn
mixed with snow: Pete's hay turned black, rotting
in his rotting loft, and he died in the poorhouse.
Peg Jones was telling how Willy's father

8

was a martinet of whitewashed tie-ups
and exact routines — while Willie can't sell his milk
because his barn would never pass inspection.
Sherm told how he and his brother Grant
took three days to muck out decades of cowshit,
black straw, and spider webs from Willy's tie-up
after H. P. Hood & Co. mailed its ultimatum.
"It took Willy one week to make it dirty as ever.
So Willy can't pay town taxes, July and December"
— he farms to feed his family: growing a garden,
churning butter the way his grandmother did,
feeding milk to pigs in order to smoke bacon,
slaughtering Holsteins to grind for hamburger —
"and every year in the fall, for taxes" (Sherman
said it aloud), "Willy sells another piece
of his daddy's farm."

                       No one spoke. Changing
the subject without changing it, Ned Buttrey
remembered how Peter Butts never cut stovewood
one winter, "so instead Pete burned old bed frames
that he hauled down from the attic, busted
rocking chairs, spinning wheels, picture frames,
and wooden chests that saved dead people's
frocks and union suits." He burned broken tables
enough to stock ten antique shops, or enough
to buy himself an oil furnace, but Pete
never thought of attic things as ANTIQUES FOR SALE.
He used up useless stuff, and the green captain's
chair his great-granddaddy dozed in burned hot,
real hot, in the rusted Glenwood kitchen range.
The last thing he burned that year — Peggy tells us;

all of us know these stories — was his outhouse.
Pete pulled it down with the nineteen twenty-four
John Deere Model D that he used for a tractor,
and sawed it up for the stove, ending
with the five-holed ancient plank, "which didn't
smell too good when it burned, is what
they say."
                    Each of us waited to add a story,
this storytelling night — it was so dark
we never saw each other's faces except
when Sherman lit a Camel; we knew each face
by its voice's shape — but before we told another,
Willy DeLord's enormous rusting Buick
sang on its dying bearings into the driveway.
(Sherm took time to mention, dropping his voice,
that Willy never changed his motor oil.
"You know that row of wrecks behind his barn . . .")
Then Willy bounced from his car, grinning, cringing
with apology, and groaning, "Gol darn it to heck!"
Victoria drove the car. Stepping out,
she followed Willy a pace behind, smiling faintly
to let you know it was Willy's predicament,
not hers. (*Willy* was hers.) "Sorry we took so long,"
she said. "We couldn't find Willy's pants."
In Victoria's headlights we watched Willy, garlanded
with rope, creep up on his loitering creatures.
He wore pinstriped gabardine trousers, muddy black
wingtip shoes, brown suspenders that rounded up
over his belly, and a Sears workshirt with many darns.
Our circle tightened to watch him as he roped
his cattle one by one, tying quick knots

around each black and white neck, his bulky body
agile and quick, until he hitched his heifers
together and straightened up — smiling, puffing,
and proud.
          By now it was midnight, three hours
after kickoff: no more traffic, which was good
because Willy had to drive his cattle now
five miles home, tapping their sluggard backs
with a birch sapling. Would Willy repair
his fence tonight? No, no. Maybe tomorrow
his seven heifers would graze Route 4 again.
     He waved goodbye, driving his cattle, as Victoria
rolled the Buick three miles an hour behind him,
headlights on bright to forewarn an oncoming car.
Now Peggy, Ned, Sherm, and the stranger made goodbyes
and headed to their machines; one by one, starters
whirred, engines caught, headlights lit, flashers
stopped flashing, and cars U-turned to vanish.
Jane went inside, to bed and electric blanket.
     Silence and darkness returned, blessed dark silence,
interrupted again by Larry Lamorte's rusty Datsun
crushing the driveway's gravel. "Dawn! Dawn! Dawn!
Who belonged to them bulls?"
                    Then I had the night
to myself. No moon, no stars, no trucks, no heifers,
no friends, no stories, and no sound: Only dark fields
and darker road, black on black, and I was alive, older
than my dark-haired father ever got to be, sleepy,
not wanting to sleep, happy, startled by happiness.

✿

The

Thirteenth

Inning

✿

1.

John Singer Sargent's *The Daughters of Edward D. Boit*
renders three reticent sisters and a silk infant
whose mother escapes citation. We study its fierce,
darkling, upright, mysterious, slick Victorian
sexuality. I called Jane "Camilla" when I
was Horace Horsecollar, and "Jennifer" while K.C.
explained baseball to Kurt Schwitters, deceased and German,
who cared nothing for baseball or my voice nattering.
As we drive home to New Hampshire, leaving the daughters
in the permanent museum, the game starts again
that ceased in the twelfth inning, although the multitude
has dispersed and Fenway Park is empty and silent.
In darkness and silence the game continues itself.

2.

When the moon rises, light standards cast eldritch shadows
on players who cast no shadows, and we observe four
transparent pitchers superimposed on each other,
from ghostly Babe Ruth past Cy Young and Smokey Joe Wood
to Parson Ted Lewis. "A thousand years a city,
a thousand years a desert," as the Hindus put it,

who recede distantly enough in antiquity
to say such things. Aphorisms, epigrams, apothegms,
and proverbs: "It is better to bend a strawberry."
In the Protestant Cemetery at Rome, near Keats,
Shelley, cats, and the pyramid of Cestius, we
find a stone marker for "Ned" Boit, father of daughters
and painter of eternal Rome. The thirteenth inning

3.

elapses as I do play-by-play for Kurt, while we
wander in dark Fenway among boxes and bleachers,
reviewing baseball's enterprise of ongoingness.
Sometimes on Sunday afternoons my father and I
drove half an hour to watch the West Haven Sailors play
baseball for a crowd innocent of television —
sometimes as Class D minors, sometimes as semipro.
Once they advertised in the *New Haven Register*
that Ralph Branca's *brother* would pitch. All losses are one:
In the Gra-Y camp I wept for loneliness; now I
dread death. At Rome, William Wetmore Story lies under
his own carved marble near Constance Fenimore Woolson.
"Never tie an honest horse to a wet rubber plant."

4.

She leapt from a balcony in Venice; Henry James
buried his friend whose suicide roared like a lion
in Lamb House: *too late, too late, too late.* As I entered
the hospital to lose the right lobe of my liver,
a fourth granddaughter was born. I thought of Boit's daughters

as Abigail followed on Emily, Allison,
and Arianna. Two weeks after I returned home,
the lesion excised, Peter Hall was born in Boston —
large, male, and redheaded like his sister Emily
and his cousin Allison, as if the beautiful
daughters of Edward D. Boit, lurking in such shadow,
were completed by a fifth and masculine presence.
"A man who touches a cabbage is seldom sorry."

5.

What may I pray for grandchildren? That the sun never
set and they never suffer? Like euphoria but
more frequent and more ineluctable, suffering
is universal and incomparable. May they
survive to cherish and make their children's children laugh,
telling them stories: When their great-grandfather Dean Smith
pulled a chain through the lumberyard and somebody asked,
"Why's Dean pulling that chain?" the boss answered, "You ever
see anybody *push* one?" Dr. Sutton performed
resection. Morphine in ICU, five minutes sleep
alternating with five minutes writhing, tubes twisted
like spider legs. I remembered my friend William Trout
and Reba, who crawled into his deathbed carefully

6.

to administer her warm body. For "writhing" read
"writing" throughout, as Hanuman and Ganesh appeared
bringing floral pots and intravenous nirvana.
When I woke in ICU — Abigail six days old —

I thrashed among seven tubes and hoses. Unable
to speak for respiring, I punched buttons to raise up
the Red Sox playing the Orioles. Who won that game?
In the cemetery at Rome, avenues of damp
and ivied marble clutter with cats and eminent
Protestant dead. Last year at the White House I observed
Ted Williams and Joe DiMaggio, both tall and gray,
leaning in the doorway and smiling while the awkward
President alluded to seasons fifty years past.

7.

"Live Free or Die." Because Queen Elizabeth the First
was short-sighted and old, courtiers could paint her cheeks
green and compliment her on a healthy complexion.
Hospitals are benign engines of paranoia:
Suffering is the privacy that accompanies
us on our cold excursion; even if it becomes
public, we examine its degree in solitude.
As I recover, spring exaggerates its vigor
and turns to baseball. Does it weary of annual
return? When Charlie Whittemore asked my grandfather,
during an August drought, if he reckoned it might rain,
Wesley Wells looked south over the blue mountain and paused
to consider the matter: "It always *has*," he said.

8.

The Spring Glen Barbershop is vacant, clean, and empty,
not even a TO LET placard leaning in the blear
plate-glass window, but the blue-red-white pole still spirals,

days and nights. Go turn the fucking thing off; go summon
Salvatore the barber back, swiveling from Sally's
— nobody knows where the switch is — oily grave of hair.

❧

It starts raining and the umpires call time. We enter a rain
delay.

In Madras, the drive to the airport should have taken half
an hour; because of the monsoon it took an hour and a quarter.
Jennifer and I were nauseated. With the windows closed, the
taxi was hot; with the windows open, the air entering the taxi
carried six-sided chunks of exhaust.

When Carlton Fisk catches, he is master at annoying hitters,
interrupting their concentration. Fisk has been called the Hu-
man Rain Delay.

The baby sitting in front is Julia Overing Boit, who became
a painter like her father; she was born in Soisy, France, 15
November 1877, and survived in Newport, Rhode Island, as late
as 1969. Jane Hubbard Boit hovers above her baby sister; she
was born in 1870 and died in Connecticut in 1955. Leaning
against the great Chinese urn is Florence, the eldest; born in
Newport in 1868, she died in Paris in 1919. On the left of the
painting is Mary Louisa Boit, born 5 June 1874 in Paris and dead
in Newport in 1945. None of them married.

Outside Bombay, a man sits on the sidewalk at noon with a
hand-operated sewing machine making shirts. Another man

pounds tin making pots and pans. A cow walks between tailor and tinker, nosing at thread but not eating. Where a baker discards a blackened edge of bread, the cow pauses to chew. Turning full circle, we see three other cows, a camel, five dogs, a pig, an elephant hauling a shrub, twelve hens, and a bullock.

During a rain delay on television we return to the studio and run highlights of the nineteen seventy-five World Series. Carlton Fisk, twenty-seven years old, hits a pitch into the screen again, ending the game in the twelfth inning. But this time something goes wrong in the mechanics of electronic reproduction: The game continues into the thirteenth inning — in total darkness, the players transparent, dead, and multiple, the audience also. . .

At the Agra railroad station, a teenage boy, bent into a semicircle, walks on all fours like an ambulatory arch, clip-clops attached to his hands. A little girl with a cute marketable smile looks up with her palm outstretched; glancing down to look away, I see that the feet of this four-year-old are as large as a basketball player's.

During a rain delay on radio, the announcers improvise their own game; no one has any idea what really happens. The game is collage, Kurt: smells of Calcutta pasted next to shreds of a liver biopsy, Ted Williams wriggling in two dimensions on a nineteen forty-one baseball card thumbtacked with a swatch of red hair swept from Salvatore's floor, catpiss from the Protestant Cemetery, Ganesh pitching with six baseballs at once, Mary Louisa Boit in pigment, and Bill Trout drunk as dirt in the empty bleachers as the rain stops.

Edward D. Boit's four pretty daughters, who are buried
not in Rome but in Connecticut, Paris, and Rhode
Island, gave this painting to the Boston Museum
thirty-seven years after Sargent painted it. Why
did none of them marry? They were representative
rich Americans who lived in Italy and France
for a hundred years while Henry James wrote about them.

9.

When Reba came to his bed at the Bayside Hospice,
Bill clasped her hands and stared steadily into her eyes,
his jaw grinding sideways as if it would dislocate;
he gazed memorizing her face for recitation
in the imminent grave. "The same goat has three blind eyes."
Kurt, for a moment let us sit behind the dugout.
Don't look, but I think that's Carl Yastrzemski coming up.
It's hard to tell, because he's as flimsy as we are.
In nineteen forty-eight, lunching in Eliot House,
I noticed two students waving their arms as they marched
the dining room's length, displaying oblongs of cardboard
they offered for sale. No one paid attention but me:
Thus I attended the Cleveland-Boston playoff, which

10.

we lost when Boudreau hit two home runs. Kurt died that year,
and like Eliot House he didn't give a goddamn.
It was a bright September afternoon, cool and clear

The Thirteenth Inning

at woeful Fenway Park; I lamented more deeply
for the lost Dodgers of Brooklyn than for Boston's team.
Last night I went to bed early, Red Sox on the coast,
and nightmared chemotherapy all night. Dread of death
consumes later life. "Witches ride when brooms go empty."
On an August weekday late in the nineteen forties
my middle-aged father drove my grandfather and me
from New Hampshire to Boston and Fenway Park, so that
Wesley Wells could watch Ted Williams address a baseball.
In eighteen ninety-eight he took the morning train south

11.

to see the Boston Nationals; Parson Ted Lewis
pitched and won. Haying, he told me stories of that game
fifty years on. In nineteen ninety-two I enter
the infusion room — where I observe the long circle
of cots and couches like sofas set for Roman feasts
with vomitoria supplied at every bedside
for bald skeletons with flesh hanging slack from their bones,
for fetal half-moons rigid in this twisted district.
Leukovorin drips into my wrist-back for two hours.
Before the registered nurse administers eighteen
cc's of 5FU into the coiled transparent
IV tubing, I take my antinausea pill.
In the infusion room, caritas tempers anguish.

12.

At my mother's house on Ardmore Street I take four naps
a day as we set her up again, at eighty-nine,
returning from another journey when she turned blue

while paramedics siren'd her to Yale–New Haven.
Jennifer freezes soup, rubs me down daily, and sees
a man at the corner of her eye who vanishes.
She recognizes the face of my father, who died
thirty-seven years ago in this airless guest room
where we sleep for a week. She says: "He looks after you."
Does he look *for* me? Today I am a dozen years
older than my father ever became. I recall
nineteen fifty-five when the Dodgers beat the Yankees
four out of seven, and my namesake died on this bed.

13.

Kurt, the players of the thirteenth inning have vanished
into white dawn. I dread that it's time to stop talking
and leave Fenway, you for your grave in England, and I
to Jennifer's passionate weeping that comforts me
in my grief at leaving her. I long to stay alive
for her careful hands, for poems, for four granddaughters
and one grandson. I know: John Singer Sargent is dead,
and Boit's daughters, and Mrs. Fiske Warren, whom I met
as an old lady with a jeweled velvet choker
while Warren Spahn pitched for the Boston Braves, whose portrait
as a beautiful middle-aged woman Sargent made.
Breathing I glue together these anthems and cutouts
of the thirteenth inning although the game is over.

14.

But not the poem. The thirteenth inning goes to fourteen
stanzas. In Pondicherry's Good Guest House the Mother's face
looked down from every wall. Stepping out into Lansdowne Street,

Kurt and I meet a visitor from another poem,
Horace Horsecollar, avid to join this last enterprise,
who metamorphoses into his muttering alter
ego, Manager Zero the cynic philosopher,
who barks as the traffic of daylight visits Kenmore Square:
"Everyone dies. Blubbering never deterred a last breath
from blurring its elegy on a redundant mirror.
The narcissist believes that his death is the only death,
and remorseless self-pity makes music of self-regard.
There is something a little wrong about the sitter's mouth.
You roll like a dog in the stinking carcass of your death."

✿

The

Old

Life

✿

Sitting in the back seat
of a nineteen thirty-five Packard
　　　with running boards, I held
my great-uncle Luther's blotchy hand.
　　　He was nine for Appomattox
and remembered the soldier
　　　boys coming home from the war.
When I pressed the skin of his hand
　　　between thumb and forefinger,
the flesh turned white as Wonder Bread.
　　　It remained indented
for a few seconds and then rose up,
　　　turning pink, flush to the surface
of his veined hairless mottled
　　　hand. Then I pressed it again.
Luther would stay old forever.
　　　I would remain six, just
beginning first grade, learning to read.

❖

　　　I remember the day.
I planned to remember it always.

For weeks we learned
the alphabet — practicing it, reciting
in unison singsong,
printing letters in block capitals
on paper with wide blue
lines, responding out loud to flash cards.
Then she said: "Tomorrow
you'll learn to read."
Miss Stephanie Ford
wrote on the blackboard
in large square letters: T H A T. "That,"
she said, gesticulating
with her wooden pointer, "is 'that.'"

Each year began
in September with a new room and a new
teacher: I started with
Stephanie Ford, then Miss Flint, Miss Gold,
Miss Sudel whom I loved,
Miss Stroker, Miss Fehm, Miss Pikosky . . .
I was announcer
at assemblies. I was elected class
president not because
I was popular but because I
was polite to grown-ups, spoke
distinctly, held my hands straight down
at my sides, and kept
my shirt tucked in: I was presidential.

Eight years in this
rectangular brick of the nineteen thirties:

If I survive to be eighty,
this box will contain the tithe
    of a long life.
In the glass case, terra is miniature:
    tiny snails and mosses,
wooden houses with sidewalks, small trees,
    and Spring Glen Grammar School.
See, pupils gather around a boy
    in black knickers
who shoots an agate, kneeling in the circle.

                            ✿

    There are miseries
of childhood that an old man's mind — alien
    in the hour of injections
and restraints, ignorant of what
    day or season it is —
will clutch to itself with angry tears.
    I wanted a Mickey Mouse
watch as much as, later in life,
    I wanted a job,
a prize, or a woman. It disappeared
    a month after my fifth
birthday, and sixty years afterward
    I grieve for it whenever
I regret something lost.

                    The year
    I was seven, at Halloween
on Harmon Street, my mother

cut up an old sheet
to make me a ghost costume. I started
down the suburban street,
stopping first at our next-door neighbors.
When I arrived at dusk,
a cocktail party to celebrate
the Yale-Dartmouth game
pounded like the sea. They gave me candy
and praised my costume —
but I felt uneasy, entering on
this ferocity of noise
and smoke; then a drunk man kneeled, teased,
poked his finger
into my nosehole, staggered, and ripped open
the whole face of my ghost.
I ran outside to my mother, red
with tears of outrage,
my children's festival ruined. Although
I would not accept
her comfort, my mother persuaded me
to wear a twenty-five-cent
mask from Kuehl's Drugs over my face
above the mangled sheet,
and I sobbed trick-or-treating from door
to door while grown-ups
repeated how original my new
costume was — Mickey's
face over the white body of a ghost.

✿

The stiffly wound celluloid
cracks when we try to uncoil it.
        These black-and-white
home movies from the depressed nineteen thirties
        show a four-year-old boy
jumping from the porch of a stucco
        house onto a scrubby lawn;
or we see the same boy at eight,
        shoveling snow with abrupt
motions, smiling self-consciously
        toward his young father's
eight-millimeter Brownie; or the same
        boy older poses,
arms rigid at his sides, wearing a child's
        fedora beside a sheepdog.

Dry film breaks; the projector
        rusts in the widow's
unvisited attic; stucco crumbles
        under vinyl siding
yet these movies continue to roll
        inside a sixty-year-old
theater where the commentator's
        voice-over regrets
the days of porches, dogs, and fedoras.

                        ✿

When my gold and white
Shetland collie Zippy died, I stayed home
        from school to weep

in the living room dark with drapes and curtains.
          Later we bought
the pedigreed Cameron of Bagaduce
          we called Cammie. Black
and white, pretty and timorous, he shook
          as I approached to pummel him —
where he lay frightened, drooling
          and trembling — and accuse him
of "trying to take Zippy's place."
          Sixty years later,
after the divorces and treacheries,
          after the deaths,
I recognize desertion, rage, and revenge.

                              ✿

          Just after I turned nine,
my great-aunt Jennie died of cancer.
          At the funeral, her brother
George felt a pain in his back
          and four months later
we buried him. Put to bed late, after
          the funeral reunion
with its straight-faced family jokes,
          I lay awake,
repeating a sentence over and over
          in my head: It was as if
I had read it in a book: "When
          he was only nine
years old, 'Death became a reality.'"

Sunday rides always ended
at Al Bott's drugstore on Elm Street
in West Haven where we sat
in booths with sundaes constructed
of Brock-Hall ice cream,
vessels of chocolate or vanilla
with nuts and spiraling
whipped cream, and each device concluded
by a maraschino cherry.
When we left from Ardmore Street
we might go anywhere:
to Long Island Sound with cottages
closed for the winter
or thronged in July; to the countryside
past woodlands, orchards, fruit
stands, dairy farms, and fields of lettuce.
I kept looking for Al's.
My father grinned as we approached, each
time by a new route
that amazed me. Each time I pondered, then
decided finally
I'd have the butterscotch this Sunday.

✿

My father wept easily,
laughed loudly when his friends teased him,
and blustered like a basso —
but *his* father was "a hard man."

H.F. was strict, handsome,
silent, and severe. When his stallion
            Skylark ran away
with my young uncle and threw him, H.F.
            galloped to a stop
beside his son's body, bellowing, "Are
            you trying to kill
the horse?" I remember the time we called
            on H.F. after church
to find him sitting upright, staring
            straight ahead without
expression, as my uncle cut his boot
            away with the carving
knife that sliced white and dark at Christmas;
            I remember the leather
curling like a black rose petal.
            That morning Skylark
slipped on clear ice that H.F. neglected
            to notice, and the horse,
falling, rolled on his leg. Jagged pink
            bone was sticking out
through H.F.'s paper-white leg skin as he
            sat stiff, resolute,
without complaint or excuse for error.

                    ✿

            There were joys, even
in Connecticut; there were miracles
            in the suburbs. Snow
still lay in patches on Ardmore's north side

when the mailman brought
the catalogue — with pages as flimsy
as a comic book's,
four colors printed askew — from the Bliss
Fireworks Company
of East Valparaiso, Indiana.
I became scholar
of smudged images: SPECIAL MAJESTIC
VENETIAN NIGHTS
and GOLDEN ETERNAL SHOWERS OF ECSTASY.
I put checks by Roman candles
and skyrockets that dropped lead
soldiers under tissue
parachutes.
My father printed out
the form in his neat letters.
When the box came I unpacked it
and lined up pinwheels and bombs,
sorting the fountains and green fire.
On the Fourth we drove
to a county where fireworks were legal
and parking on a dirt
road after dark flared our paradise
of fire.
The next day
I began right away to plan ahead
for next year, foreseeing
fireworks always with my young father,
slender rockets unpacking
their quick shoots of burning petals,
green gold, as we two

became one person, ecstatic and joint,
    blossoming together
into smoke that enlarged and expired.

        ✿

    My father's new barometer
broke the moment he nailed it
    on the sunroom wall:
The damned thing predicted a HURRICANE.
    By noon the wind
was homicidal. From the fifth-grade windows
    pasted with cut-out leaves,
we watched tree branches tangle and snap
    like dogs in a dogfight
as our teachers conferred with Miss Baum
    who spoke to the director.
Then the telephone fell silent.
    They dismissed us at two o'clock,
the storm at its worst. Walking
    down Thornton Street
I heard a crash behind me: A maple lay
    with limbs still shaking.
Then for a week no school, no water, no
    electricity, no cars
or trolleys. We bicycled all
    day through the suburban
streets among dead wires from broken poles,
    past the domed elms fallen
crisscross, oaks with green acorns, maples
    huge and splintered, great roots
scribbled upward, writhing in stillness.

Bored in the back seat,
eleven, I daydreamed in the prose style
of someone eleven years old.
If I should declare, "I crave
excitement," my father
would answer, "I know just what you crave,"
and swing the car around
— I watched the back of his thirty-six-
year-old neck and his thin
hair neatly cut; I watched my skinny
mother wearing a hat
and earrings — to head it toward the lewd
honkytonk paradise
of Savin Rock: Jimmy's hotdogs split
and fried; the Tunnel of Love
with its wriggling darkness and long
terminal drop into
water; the House of Horror; the Wheel
that tilted us upside
down, screaming in ebullient terror;
the breathless roller coaster . . .
At last I could not hold back: "I
crave excitement," I said.
"I know just what you crave," he answered
— with an irony
I hadn't credited my father with
or practiced a comeback for —
"and it's something that costs money."

✿

My aunt the English teacher,
who wrote verses for Hallmark cards
    and looked like my mother
only younger and plumper, took me
    walking in the woods
when I was five. She stirred me with stories
    about a one-eyed
giant outwitted by a clever Greek
    sailor; about a wooden
puppet whose nose elongated
    when he told a lie.
Aunt Liz was pretty, generous, moody,
    and fierce in affections
and desires. I cherished her. When I
    was eleven or twelve,
one summer when she was without love
    and lonely in her thirties,
she visited the farm. She took
    to crawling into
my bed for a cuddle as I woke up
    until one morning,
as she squeezed herself against me, Liz flushed
    and leapt from bed, saying
I was grown up now; she was sorry.

❀

When her young sister
married, Liz was still single after years
    of falling for this
handsome egotistical playboy or

that one. She made up her mind
that she would accept the next man
      who proposed marriage.
Thus she acquired Uncle Emmanuel —
      perpetual chatterer
of unspeakable awkwardness,
      nervous giggles,
and inane mortifying unfunny jokes,
      who became the yearly
visible sore on Thanksgiving's face;
      who deadened decades
of Christmas. Beautiful Aunt Liz resigned
      herself to accepting
the fate she contracted for, and smiled
      relentlessly, without
import, until her arteries fouled.
      On her deathbed she told me —
pale, old, and darling; skeptical
      about messages of pain —
"I don't believe this heart business."

                    ✿

      The northernmost Thimble,
off Guilford, the island divided
      itself from the mainland
by a channel with a private bridge,
      gates, and German shepherds.
My uncle Arthur bought it when things
      were cheap in nineteen
thirty-six. Only two years afterward

the hurricane wiped out
his trees, shrubs, garden, and sea wall; but
      the Victorian house, "built
to withstand hurricanes," withstood
      a hurricane.
Afterward, all during the American
      Century
(1945–1965; R I
      P), while the Dairy
prospered and everybody's sensible
      utilities brought in
a prudent five percent, my uncle
      sold lots — subdividing
an old quarry he bought on the shore
      across the bridge —
to rich friends from New Haven. He erected
      a cabana and bought
a cabin cruiser. From the six-room
      house on Ardmore Street
we drove to the island on Saturdays
      to join the continuous
party: badminton, croquet, beer,
      hotdogs, wisecracks,
every summer all summer. The sun never
      wavered from its noon
in the permanent Connecticut sky.

                              ✿

      In Spring Glen, nineteen
forty-one was melancholy. Were all

these years so sad?
My father hated his job at the Dairy,
        working for his father,
and came home weeping. When my mother
        recovered from an operation,
she took to bed again
        with a "nervous stomach."
That Christmas we experimented:
        Our window candles had blue bulbs;
the lights on the tree burned blue.
        We sat in the dark house,
blue in its hollow darkened by shrubs
        and trees, in the blue
darkness of the den, blue gazing at blue.

                    ✿

        In the cellar at the long
workbench I sat alone, after
        school, three hours at a stretch.
I cut balsa struts and glued tail parts
        together; I shrunk
tissue paper over skeletal
        wings and fuselages; —
but every model airplane I built
        fell apart or crashed.
When I failed I tried again, opening
        the new kit without hope,
slicing balsa with a single-edged
        Gem razor, my jaws
clenched in my resolve to rise in the air

over the lawns and small
garages of Hamden and Spring Glen.

✿

When I was twelve I bused
alone from Hamden to New Haven
to go to the movies,
to worship at the Church of Corpses:
The Wolf Man in brute
carnations, *Frankenstein, Dracula, Bride
of Frankenstein.* The boy
next door's name was Billy Harris, three
years older; he said, "If you like
that sort of stuff, you should read
Edgar Allan Poe."
With this advice my life began. I tried
writing poems and stories
imitating Poe. Because I
constructed myself,
I consulted Hervey Allen's thousand-
page biography
Israfel, which made much of young Edgar
reading Keats and Shelley
at fourteen. I saved my allowance
to buy, for a dollar
twenty-five, the Modern Library
Keats and Shelley, and read it
straight through, resolute — and two years
smarter than Poe — to script
the home movie of the chosen life.

Seeking without
success the admiration of glamorous
        high school cheerleaders,
I sought generic fame. I failed at sports
        and took up poetry.
Regretfully, after reading Keats,
        Yeats, Dickinson, H.D.,
Hart Crane, Frost — always in love, fickle —
        I gave up the bobby-soxed
girls I loved who kicked from white skirts
        for poems that outshone
like the sun my nympholept moonshine.

✿

As a Boy Scout
I never owned a uniform. At fourteen
        I went to Scout meetings
as a way to get out of the house.
        Talking one night
with David Johnstone — uniformed, ironic,
        sophisticated, First Class,
sixteen — we proved ourselves members
        of the Teenage Ambition
Club, in whom "the desire to be
        extraordinary,"
as the Autocrat of the Breakfast
        Table put it, "is
commonplace." I bragged that in my high school

study hall that morning
I had written a poem. Dave's eyes
        quickened with passion.
"Do you write *poems?*" he said. "Yes," I said.
        "Do you?" Pulling
himself up, he uttered a noble sentence
        that dictated the rest
of my life: "It is my profession."

                    ✿

        Summers at the farm
with the old people, freed from the suburbs,
        I hayed three loads
every afternoon. Mornings I set aside
        for writing and reading:
one summer, Shakespeare and the Bible.
        Before noon dinner
I wandered in the cut-over hayfield
        to lie on my back,
loosening my soul into the running
        clouds and tall white pine,
into the hay-bearing New Hampshire land.
        I lived for poetry
at my brown table, Prospero's tune,
        and in the clovery
wind that touched me, loading the hayrack.

                    ✿

        In Hamden High School
I betrayed my class, rejecting Spring Glen,

both the two-bit side
of Whitney Avenue with our six-room
house and the half-dollar side
where professors from Yale hired maids.
My friends were from State Street
instead — Willy Kovacs, whose parents
fled Béla Kun; Fred
Majyk, whose father cooked for a diner;
the twins Sam and Frank
Martino, who lived at East Rock Park where
their father tended
the rose garden. We started our own frat,
as we called it, imitating
the rich kids from Spring Glen with
their cars and girls.
We read the dirty parts of *Studs Lonigan*
and got drunk. For a party,
we bought one bottle each of gin,
rum, ale, vodka, sherry,
rye whiskey, and Chianti. Staying
with Fred, I vomited
from his bedroom onto the porch roof.
"Is that why he visits you?"
asked Fred's mother. "To get so drunk?"

✿

At my prep school
I birddogged the girlfriend of a popular
student, a refugee boy
named Giles, when she visited him
from Northampton

for a dance weekend. She flirted; I flirted,
    as cruel as she was.
We danced the whole night. At six A.M.
    we sneaked from our rooms
to meet, to kiss and rub on each other.
    When she left, my shabby
triumph dwindled. Nobody told me,
    but I heard the whispers,
and later was allowed to observe
    the membership cards
— hand-lettered, awkward, but memorable —
    that allowed me
reasonable cause for the paranoia
    so useful in literary
work: THE WE-HATE-DON-HALL CLUB.

❀

At Exeter I subscribed
to the weekly tabloid *Worker*
    which I read, never
in the privacy of my single room
    in red brick Hoyt Hall,
but in the dormitory's dim buttroom
    underground, where I
spread it wide open and held it high, so
    that all the sixteen-
year-old lifelong right-wing Republicans,
    whose fathers considered
Roosevelt red and doubtless a Jew,
    could observe my

periodical of choice.
                    Later Harvard
          seemed as Commie as I was:
I went to hootenannies, where
          it was rumored you
could get laid, and was the youngest recruit
          in the Cambridge
Citizens' Committee to Aid the Strikers
          at Squires Meatpacking
Plant. We offered the local CIO
          our help with picketing.
The union boss, looking us over,
          decided it was best
we didn't join the line, with posters
          claiming solidarity.
"The boys are a little jumpy."

                    ❖

          Every night I drank beer
at Cronin's with my friends, but retired
          by ten o'clock. An alarm
woke me at six; shaggy with sleep,
          unshaved and uncombed,
with a black binder of poetry wedged
          under my arm, I plugged
up hill to Harvard Square and a booth
          at Albiani's, black
coffee, Danish, a lined pad, and my
          Parker 51. I crossed
old words out and substituted

words that probably
I would cross out in their turn tomorrow.
        After two hours
I walked back to Eliot House and breakfast
        with the day ahead of me:
lectures, Grolier, reading, Cronin's.

                        ✿

        If Frank was a bird,
he was a bird of prey. In memory,
        it seems that I spent
most of my sophomore year at parties
        gossiping with Frank,
who finished every verbal sortie with
        a last word emitted
in the ruthless melody of camp.
        Foolish with Pickwick Ale,
I tried to keep up, and once archly
        compared him to Oscar Wilde.
With eyebrows that hovered to strike,
        he delivered his lethal
sentence: *"You're* the *type* that would *sue!"*

                        ✿

        The proprietor
of the Grolier Book Shop on Plympton Street
        was an old man
with a bump on his forehead. All day each day
        he sat on a spilling

sofa with his back to the storefront
    window — grumpy, insulted
by students who asked for textbooks.
    All day poets came calling
to gossip with Gordon Cairnie,
    sometimes even
to buy a book. A *1927*
    Daily Reminder
as ravaged and durable as Gordon's
    cranky affections
kept his records: what he owed publishers;
    what poets owed him. "Thanks
be to railroad stock," he liked to say.
    His voice made a tune:
"Atchison, Topeka, and Santa Fe."

                   ✿

On the *Advocate*
in nineteen forty-eight, we argued all
    night about whether
a poem was decent enough to print.
    John Ashbery sat
in a chair, shelling pistachio nuts;
    Robert E. Bly wore a three-
piece suit and a striped tie; Kenneth
    Koch was ever sarcastic.
Once as we pasted an issue
    together we discovered
a blank page and teased Ashbery
    to give us a new poem.

John disappeared to Dunster House.
      When he dawdled back
with his lines about fortunate Alphonse,
      we admired it
and pasted it up. Later he admitted
      that he had gone back
to his room and improvised the poem
      on his Olivetti.
When I told him the story forty
      years later, John laughed.
"Yes," he said, sighing. "I took longer then."

❖

      When I came home for Christmas
halfway through college, my girlfriend
      from Simmons wrote me
a note: She'd had her period. Of course
      my mother read the letter,
and my father with a broad smile
      — anxious, loving, terrified —
suggested we have a talk. "One
      thing," he said to begin with.
"You mustn't go back to Boston
      for the New Year's party."
It was A Turning Point in our lives.
      I knew it; he knew it.
Our hearts thudded; tears cornered our eyes.
      I Dug In My Heels;
he Lost His Composure — telling me that
      "if you go to the party,
you will be kicking your mother's

body." They drove me to Boston
— reproach by kindness — and next
        morning at breakfast,
after two hours' sleep, I was filial
        and affectionate, tired,
happy, smelling love on my fingers.

                    ✿

        At college in my junior year,
I had a nervous breakdown,
        or so I told Dr.
Coluccio in a long letter
        I typed at my desk
in Eliot House. Troubled, exhausted,
        fretful, I explained
that I needed to quit school, certainly
        to get away from Harvard.
I spoke in *desperation:* I
        couldn't sleep or study
or write; my life was impossible,
        painful, *insupportable . . .*
I didn't tell him I'd broken
        with Freda, then gone with
Rosalind and split up with her, then
        Priscilla. I typed,
making many errors, and intended
        to hand-deliver my letter
right then, but when I finished,
        I felt overwhelmingly
sleepy.
        I woke after two hours

calm and cheerful.
I read it over, then crumpled the letter.

✿

In fall of my last year,
a notice arrived bringing Greetings
        and an invitation
to the armory in New Haven
        on a Friday afternoon.
My Connecticut physician
        composed a letter describing
my migraine headaches. An old
        doctor in a brown suit
glanced over it, showed it to someone,
        and declared, "He's *in*,"
to the room at large.
                        Naked, cold, wretched,
        we moved among corpsmen
with their stethoscopes and chill fingers.
        When we had finished,
Sergeant Piacek called nine men by name,
        to dress and leave.
I wanted desperately not to exchange
        Harvard for Korea,
yet pitied the rejected men. We
        remaining stood meaty
and shameful while Sergeant Piacek
        called us in gangs
of five to congratulate us on making
        1-A. With each group,

the Sergeant clapped one new soldier stoutly
    on the shoulder, saying
a word or two: "Hall, you're my lead scout."
    The next day, General
Hershey announced student deferments.

          ❖

    My last spring at college
I bought a beat-up wire recorder
    and with my friends
invented a radio quiz program called
    The Giant Broom.
Each contestant told a lachrymose story.
    Murmuring his sympathy,
the MC would explain the rules:
    "If you answer
the question correctly, you get a million
    dollars tax-free; but if
you fail, the Giant Broom will sweep you
    into our Incinerator
where you will burn to death for
    the entertainment
of our studio audience." The questions:
    "Who is Sylvia?" "How
can we know the dancer from the dance?"
    "Oh, I'm *so* sorry . . ."
As the Broom swished, we recorded screams of
    terror and agony,
as well as applause from spectators.
    We played the game

The Old Life

all night, in the weeks before graduation,
    waiting for honors,
graduate school, partnership in Morgan
    Stanley, or
possibly a police action in Korea.

✿

When I asked Wallace
Stevens permission to reprint poems
    he published in the *Advocate,*
he acceded with a note
    that set me thinking: "Some
of one's early things give one the creeps."

Later I went up to him
at a brunch before The Game, where
    he stood with friends
from Hartford Accident and Indemnity.
    I deferred to the poet;
the businessman blushed and muttered.
    I asked if he could stay
in town through Monday; the *Advocate*
    was giving a party
for Mr. Eliot — "or maybe
    for you both?" "Shit," he said,
"fuck. Got to get back to the office."

✿

Mr. Eliot at sixty-
three — Nobel Laureate and Czar —

54

kindly suggested
that I drop by his office at Faber's
in London on my way
to Oxford. In dazed preparation,
I daydreamed agendas
for our conversation. At his desk,
the old poet spoke
quietly of "the poetic drama,"
and "our literary
generations," as if I had one.
After an hour, he scraped
his chair back. I leapt up, and he leaned
in the doorway
to improvise a parting word. "Let me see,"
he said. "Forty years
ago I went from Harvard to Oxford,
now you from Harvard
to Oxford. What advice may I give you?"
He paused the precise
comedian's millisecond as I
reflected on the moment,
and then with his exact lilting
English melody inquired:
"Have you any long underwear?"

✤

At the depot I told
the cabby "Christ Church College." Stooping
to pick up my suitcases
in front of Christopher Wren's Tom

The Old Life

Tower, I was confronted
by a kind elderly gentleman,
        as I interpreted him,
wearing a suit and a bowler,
        who spoke to me with firmness:
"Your bags, sir" — his words exactly —
        "will be delivered
to your room." I followed a similar
        figure through Tom Quad,
past the cauliflower column by the Hall,
        past the rotten stone
of Old Library, to the groined entrance
        of Meadow Buildings 4.
As I inspected my new quarters
        I was saluted by
a sprightly, handsome young Englishman
        who bowed and destroyed
my remaining composure by claiming,
        cheerfully, without
apparent shame, "I am your servant, sir."

                        ❁

        When we graduated
we voted Bill Hapgood First Marshal
        of the Class of '51.
Bill went off to graduate school,
        and his twin brother
Parkman to Korea, where he was killed
        six months later
rolling on a grenade to save his platoon.

There was a posthumous
Congressional Medal of Honor
        as I learned how to hold
my sherry at Christ Church, studying
        Oxford one-upmanship
with Etonians just mustered out
        from the Green
Howards. I defended my nation by insult
        against resentful
former soldiers of empire in the Hall
        of the House founded
by Cardinal Wolsey, completed by
        Henry Tudor, whose
Holbein portrait we ate porridge under.
        Seven PLC classmates
died that first year, "quit for the next,"
        and for our twenty-fifth
reunion, where I drank beer with Bill
        and other old friends,
some heavy with many honors, some not.

✿

The gate under Tom Tower
closed at midnight. After a night of
        gin from the bottle,
I tried climbing into college and fell
        into the drainage ditch
behind Veterans' Memorial
        Garden. I lay in the muck
— content, resting — until two young

constables hauled me out
and stood me upright, drenched and choking,
in my new tailor-made
suit with a vest from London. Gently
they tendered me to the back
gate of the House and rang the night
porter's bell. Sleepy,
fully dressed with his bowler, Mr. Jenks
blinked as the constables
announced that I claimed to be "Donald
'all." With expert
weariness he sighed, "So 'e is. So 'e is."

✿

In the nineteen forties
I wore my Blue Notes down to scratches
and visited the Savoy
Saturday nights to hear Wild Bill,
Vic Dickenson, Teddy Bunn,
Pops Foster, and Big Sid. The spring
of nineteen fifty-two,
in Paris, I hoarded black-market
francs to hire a table
at Vieux Columbier for *le jazz
hot de* Sidney Bechet.
Afternoons, I sauntered past Hôtel
Montana on Rue Saint-Benoît
where the man from New Orleans
tilted back on a wooden
chair by the door. When I tried out

"Good afternoon," he agreed.
In the dark nightclub he played "Dear
Old Southland"
and "Summertime" on clarinet and soprano
sax. One Pernod warmed
beside me as I heard Sidney Bechet
announce in his Cajun
French, "*Et maintenant,* 'Muscat Ramble.'"

❧

If I lived in Peckwater
Quad a thousand years, tended by
scouts and bedders
in luxury of service undiminished
by the need to walk
half a mile to a bathtub, I wouldn't
comprehend the interclass
manners of Oxford. The servant
for the JCR
at the House — a lean bespectacled man
of some years who wore
black, never smiled, and carried a dozen
teacups without
permitting any to rattle — called himself
Arthur Hall. Idly,
I mentioned that my father's brother bore
the same appellation,
then watched astonished as color drained
from the already gray
obsequious face of Arthur Hall,

who mumbled his
sincere gratitude for my condescension
and fled to his pantry.
I heard the sound of saucers rattling.

*

It was the year when
everybody got married. I was there
with my tall beautiful
bride when Tom McElroy went berserk.
When he reached
the getaway car after the silk reception,
Tom found his ushers
gathered to decorate the Cadillac
the usual way — with *Just
Married,* pie plates, ribbons, and straw.
He was furious. He rushed
forward to kick Geoff, who padlocked
tire chains to an axle,
then swung at me, who sprayed silver paint.
When we all understood
that Tom was drunk or crazy — drunk *and*
crazy — we stepped back.
He sped off toward the airport, *Just Married,*
Maggie relentlessly
and appropriately blubbering
beside him as he
grumbled in a continuous outrage
while they started their
decade's trip toward the usual divorce.

✿

Thomas was thirty-eight,
rumpled and fat, when I slept over
     at the Boat House after
swilling through Laugharne's pubs. As we sat
     drinking one last
Whitbread, I changed the subject to poetry.
     Quickly I learned: His poems
depressed him. He knew what he'd done,
     what he hadn't done,
and that he was done for. As I chatted
     about critics,
I laughed at someone who pontificated
     in a quarterly about
"The Death Wish in Dylan Thomas."
     Young and careless, I asked,
"Who wants to die?" Behind his heavy
     lids, Dylan said that *he* did.
"Why?" I asked him. "Oh, for the change."

✿

Edwin and Willa Muir
translated Kafka, working in Prague
     for the British Council.
Edwin reviewed novels for the *Times,*
     did talks for the BBC,
and advised a small publisher.
     They lived by their wits
as Edwin made poems. When I met them,
     they were sixty-odd,

tender and generous. I asked Willa
how it was to be old,
and she said it was "surprisingly
good . . . except that one
will need to close the eyes of the other."

✿

My mother said, "Of course,
it may be nothing, but your father
has a spot on his lung."
That was all that was said: My father
at fifty-one could never
speak of dreadful things without tears.
When I started home,
I kissed his cheek, which was not our habit.
In a letter, my mother
asked me not to kiss him again
because it made him sad.
In two weeks, the exploratory
revealed an inoperable
lesion.
The doctors never
told him; he never asked,
but read *The Home Medical Guidebook.*
Seven months later,
just after his fifty-second birthday
— his eyesight going,
his voice reduced to a whisper, three days
before he died — he said,
"If anything should happen to me . . ."

When I first taught freshman
English, girls leaned over their papers
    so that their breasts nudged
my tweedy shoulder; I walked home trembling
    to drink bourbon. Teaching
was risky: My student Stephen Bliss
    showed up at five o'clock
just as I was ending office hours
    to show his bandaged
wrist. "They let me out," he said eagerly,
    "so that I could catch you
before you left." Whiskey that evening
    allowed me skepticism:
Stephen slashed his wrist for show-and-tell.
    But two years afterward
I learned that the boy had hanged himself
    in his grandmother's cellar
at Charlevoix; some of the girls,
    I found later, actually
took their clothes off and lay back.

                    ✿

    I had taught for six months
when Robert Graves came to Ann Arbor.
    "The name is Robert,"
he told me at the Union when I tried
    formal address.
Ashamed to be a professor, I told him

I envied the way
he wrote prose for a living. He asked me,
    "Have you ever tried?"
As we finished our coffee and ice cream
    in the ratty student
cellar, I asked, "But how do you write
    so much?" Graves published
three books a year — poems, novels, pieces
    for *Punch,* crank
anthropology — while I dozed through my twenties.
    Robert Graves never lacked
an answer: "The twenty-minute nap."
    When I protested,
he repeated, "The twenty-minute nap."

        ✿

    At Michigan games
early in the fall when Andrew was four,
    I explained each play
in detail: single wing, quick kick, Statue
    of Liberty, off-tackle
slant. It took me a while to note
    Andrew's resolute patience.
"Do you mind me saying all this?"
    I asked. He answered,
"No," and, after a pause for politeness,
    continued, saying, "I'd
rather you didn't, but I don't *mind.*"

        ✿

In nineteen fifty-nine,
in Thaxted with my young family,
        the priest was Father Jack
Putterhill — musician, Communist, wag,
        and Morris dancer.
Village Tories crossed the street to avoid
        meeting him on the pavement
but he taught their children to dance,
        sing, and play the violin
when the parents weren't looking.
        He told stories: how,
in the thirties, he sat with town burghers
        in the guild hall, doling
out the dole, while unemployed workers
        in the loft above
rang out "The Internationale." Nervous
        merchants asked Father
Jack if he might ask the boys to sing less
        noisily. Jack climbed
the ladder to join them — as he told us —
        whispering, "Fine, boys,
fine. Excellent. But louder now, *louder.*"

                    ✿

After dinner at Crispi's
we drove around Rome. "There's the *scene* —
        of the *crime,*" he said
as we passed a building, in the accent
        or melody that sounded
like W. C. Fields. "Where you broadcast

the talks?" "Where I *gave* 'em —
the *scripts.*" When he couldn't remember
        the way to Hadrian's
tomb, he sank back in diffident woe.
        But when, with his yellow
Confucian scarf slung on his shoulders,
        he bought gelati
and we strolled a piazza together,
        old Ezra Pound cocked
his lionish head like a gallantman
        captain of mercenaries
hired by a Sforza.
                        Answering
        my knock the first day
I arrived from Thaxted, he addressed me
        in small bursts like sporadic
gunfire: "Mr. Hall — you have *come*
        — all the *way* — from *England* —
and you *find* me — nothing but *fragments.*"

                    ✿

        Because I was always
busy writing when we were home, my
        son and I did our best
talking in the car. When he was six
        we drove from Thaxted
to Cambridge to do the laundry, and I
        told him about
running the 440 at Exeter, how
        I raced in a JV meet

against a runner named Bill Best
        from Dover High School
whom I determined to beat. I sprinted
        for the pole and was timed
at the 220 mark two seconds
        faster than I ran
the 220 by itself in practice,
        but blacked out as I rounded
the goal posts on the final turn,
        finishing dead last,
and vomited behind the stadium.
        Later the old doctor
said that my heart was enlarged (untrue)
        and switched my sport
from track to marksmanship.
                        I told the story
        excitedly, eloquent
or proud with remembered failure —
        and looked across
the car seat to see my son's face wet with tears
        and heard his passionate
voice implore me to practice again
        for the 440, running
on footpaths among Essex farms,
        to approach the finish
line kicking, Bill Best a yard ahead.

                        ✿

When I interviewed Henry
Moore's old friends for a *New Yorker*

profile, Edward
Bantam invited me to dine at his house.
    I brought whiskey. The old
man remembered forty years back, young
    art-student roommates
arrived from Yorkshire to London, sculptor
    and portrait painter:
Edward Bantam's portrait of Moore's mother
    hung in the dining room
at Henry Moore's house.
                    But Ned Bantam
    at forty converted
to surrealism. I looked; I looked
    away. He told
anecdotes of friendship in bohemia
    as we drank Glenfiddich
until his head fell forward, he wept,
    and complained that Henry
remembered nothing of the old times,
    but had to send me,
a stranger, to ask him about the years
    they worked side by side
for fame that would divide them forever.

                    ✿

    Moore was sixty when I
met him. Before tea — when he had worked
    eight hours on maquettes,
waxes, an eight-foot reclining figure
    in elmwood, and a

monumental two-part shaped like the skull
        of an elephant — we played
Ping-Pong. He was quick, resourceful,
        wiry, competitive,
thirty years older, and I beat him.
        When I smashed the ball
to his backhand, before he could swing his
        paddle to meet it,
he swatted the ball back over the net
        with his naked left hand.
"That counts," he said quickly, "doesn't it?"

        He liked to repeat
advice that Rodin gave to young sculptors:
        "If you're working
on a maquette, and it doesn't go right, don't
        keep picking at the clay,
making little changes here and there.
        Drop it on the floor.
See what it looks like then." And he liked it
        that Rodin remembered
tips from the craftsman who counseled him
        when they labored
together in an artisan's shop. "Rodin,"
        said Adolph Constant
to the apprentice, "your leaves are too flat.
        Make some with edges pointing
straight up at you. Never think of
        a surface except
as the extremity of a volume."
                . . .

The last time I saw him,
he was eighty. I asked him, "Henry,
     what is the secret
of life?" He didn't hesitate; he said:
     "The secret is to devote
your whole life to one ambition.
     Concentrate everything
you know, everything you can summon,
     to accomplish this
one desire. But remember: Choose something
     you can't do!" He laughed
and coughed, shifting his weight in the wheelchair.

❉

     At the opening
cocktail party of *Playboy*'s conference,
     "Great Young American
Novelists," Styron and Bourjaily
     speculated about
procedures or engines by which they
     might rectify certain
reviewers. Their words exemplified
     the spirit of this
writers' weekend, which ended when Nelson
     Algren stubbed his cigar
on a teacher of English's grand
     piano, all the great
young writers took off in a taxi
     to pick up coeds
(returning shortly without coeds, drunk,

and thirsty), and
my friend Floyd the old novelist with bad luck
    hurtled down two flights
of stairs to remainder his collarbone.

✿

Every Friday there were
at least two cocktail parties, and on
    Saturday four or five.
I went to them all. At each the same
    student bartenders
and waitresses passed the same hors d'oeuvres
    to the same people. Midnight,
we straggled off, stuffing our mouths
    with a last sausage
or artichoke heart, drunkenly driving
    to the City Bar
with its trio of jazz musicians, where
    we ate enormous hamburgers.
Then I drove home drunk, and drove
    babysitters home drunk,
and fell into the Saturday night
    coma until noon
on Sunday, the *New York Times* and bagels,
    a late afternoon date
for tennis followed by another
    cocktail party or supper —
for a decade of Rusty Nails,
    children, hangovers,
babysitters, love affairs, melted cheese.

The names I put to feelings
contradicted the feelings. (I
    malefacted
benignancy.) For the first half of my life,
    my forehead wore an erratum
slip: "For 'love' read 'rage' throughout."

✿

At his last Ann Arbor
reading — at the age of eighty-eight,
    months before he died — Robert
Frost nodded, smiled, waved, and trembled
    while two thousand people
stood applauding. Drinking 7-Up
    afterward, he told us
that Ezra Pound was effeminate,
    Yeats talked bunkum,
and Roethke was jealous of other poets.
    When he shuffled
from green room to limo, a crowd of students
    gathered to catch
sight of him. He V'd his arms like Eisenhower
    and told them, "Remember me."
In the back of the limousine,
    Frost shook his head:
"To think that I wanted only to lodge four
    lines somewhere, to stick . . . !"
While I watched, his face — full of victory —

reversed suddenly
to guilty sorrow: "But we were so poor."

⌗

When my daughter was four
or five, she acquired football language
    from sitting on my lap
as I watched the Detroit Lions. One
    Sunday night, as I put her
to bed, she asked me to perform
    "unnecessary roughness,"
by which she meant tickling. Every
    night thereafter we
roughhoused at bedtime, until the divorce.

On Wednesdays we had from six
through supper, the night, and breakfast;
    I put her to bed
with our old roughness, madcap and careful.
    On Mondays I picked her up
when school let out at two-fifteen,
    and we drove to a park
near Ann Arbor which had the best swings,
    then to the Homestyle
Hamburger, then back to her mother's house
    for a story at bedtime.
In my room I cracked the ice tray.

⌗

At the university,
the faculty spent its weekends
        throwing itself dinner
parties, introduced by seminars
        in the culture of Scotch
on the rocks. I enjoyed these revels,
        except when an eminent
senior professor of English,
        stiff with collegiality,
asked me, as if his question
        required no answer, "And
how is our great poet this evening?"

❀

That time I needed
to order thirty-eight veal chops for the
        Society's dinner,
and figured that nobody would stock
        so many, I asked
Druzetich the butcher, "Can I order
        ahead?"
                "Sure,"
he answered, reckless with idiom, "no problem,"
        and grinned with Hungarian
competence: "What kind of a head?"

❀

It was one of the marches.
My fourteen-year-old son's hair blazed

down to his shoulders.
We boarded the night bus in Ann Arbor
for Washington D.C.
where we carried the names of dead men
and filed under the high
windows of the Justice Department
where John and Martha
discussed "revolution." At noon we stopped
to lunch at the Press Club
with newspaper friends, where I showed off
my beard, beads, and buttons.
As we entered the brass dining room
I spied Mike Dale,
whom I'd known at school, a Washington writer
I'd never much cared for.
He cut me dead, irritating me,
until the old columnist
we ate with squinted to make out
the face of Mike's
companion over lunch — who was Ron Ziegler.
When Nixon's press
secretary departed, Mike approached us,
hand outstretched, smiling,
admiring my beads and Andrew's long hair.

❧

In nineteen sixty-seven
I taught English at Michigan
and my student Carl
Oglesby took me to a meeting of

The Old Life

SDS leaders who argued
doctrinal Marxism while they
    pursued righteousness
through jargon. My mind wandered as I sat
    looking on, attempting
to seem interested, but my mouth
    twitched.
                Carl was intelligent
and loved Yeats. "Come on," Carl called me.
    "Let's go sit
in the corner, Don, and talk about poetry."

                    ✿

With a drink in my hand
and my mouth turned down, I sat with Min
    and Bill looking
at the television picture in July
    of nineteen sixty-nine
as my life emptied like a bottle
    on its side, glug glug
glug. In two months I would turn forty-one:
    Hopeless, divorced,
abandoned, without love or my children, I
    understood that my losses
were my own contrivance. I sat
    drinking gin while snowy
Neil Armstrong fixed his indefinite
    heavy enormous boots
to a ladder's rungs and wobbled down
    toward the moon's scattered

rubble and boring surface. Who cared? If
      he spoke from a sound-
stage in Arizona, who the fuck cared?

          ✿

      It was an Equity
production. At the start of the play
      James Whitmore turned
to watch as I delivered my seven words,
      then had me machine-gunned
to death, on a portion of the stage
      representing fantasy.
I took my own good time to die.
      Because I played a critic
killed by a writer, newspapers
      led their reviews with me
— "Nice notices," the real actors said —
      and the scene stopped the show.
After two nights, James Whitmore wondered
      if maybe this interruption
at the top hurt the play's rhythm.
      "Tonight," he said, "I won't
look at you when you fall." Sure enough,
      he cut the laugh by two thirds
for the rest of the run.
              Backstage,
      I waited two hours
in the dressing room for the curtain call.
      "You don't have to stay,"
one actress told me. "You could just go home."

When I started with Dr.
Frolich, I cherished his white hair,
　　　his bated Viennese
accent, his ironical eyebrows,
　　　and his silence. If I
confessed to an "oral fixation,"
　　　he avowed bewilderment
as to what my words might mean. When
　　　I said that sometimes
I caught myself noting the quantity
　　　of a bowel movement,
eyebrows fluttered: "*Caught?*" he repeated.
　　　Some of my poet friends
accuse me of paying too much mind
　　　to dead metaphors.
Six years later, when we terminated —
　　　after I had abandoned
all jargon, after a thousand
　　　boxes of Kleenex — I had learned
to walk through his door letting
　　　feelings and associations
out; and he had learned to talk:
　　　"One day," he said lightly,
"you will be able to love someone."

✿

My son and I sat in
right-field upper-deck front-row box seats
　　　where left-handed pull

78

hitters hit home runs. It wasn't until
       the seventh inning
of the second game that our Norman Cash
       lifted one up:
                    The ball
grew larger as it closed, like the moon
       approaching Apollo's
astronauts that summer. I stuck out
       my empty left hand
— there was an El Producto in my right —
       and the ball banged
against my palm, a smack clearly audible
       to the whole ballpark,
before bouncing to the first deck. My hand
       puffed up, flushed like my face,
as I stood and bowed to the crowd's cheers.

       When we had lost both games,
my son and I drove in silence to
       his mother's place. Back
in my room, I drank bourbon red-handed.

                    ✿

       Reluctantly I left
the young woman to hitchhike westward
       on the Chicago turnpike
after her three-day social call
       on the lam from trashing
a draft board in Pennsylvania
       by pouring lamb's blood

obtained from a butcher with a pigtail
      over the records.
When I returned, I found a man on my
      doorstep wearing a brown
fedora above a brown suit with
      brown shoes. As we finished
talking, he stood stiffly, and removed
      from his coat a printed
card, and read me the Harboring Act.

✿

      In June when I was leaving
Ann Arbor, I took Jane Kenyon
      to a blues concert,
then flew to Hollywood to do a book
      I never finished.
I stayed at the Hollywood–La Brea
      Motel, dined at
Hamburger Heaven, paced over Boulevard
      stars at night, then sat tight
to drink whiskey and watch bad movies.
      Returning months later,
it was Jane again I telephoned.

      We looked into each
other's eyes, then nervously looked away,
      in dread of love's
outrage and abandonment. Once at midnight
      as we sat together
in my living room, the old mother

cat slithered through the port
with her stomach ripped open. We rushed
to the vet for stitches,
shots, and reassurance. When we brought
the groggy cat back home,
for the first time we spoke of marriage.

❦

The judge was decent, but
judge's chambers were judge's chambers,
yellow and municipal
in downtown Ann Arbor. My kids
were dear and anxious.
Jane's brother and sister-in-law, mother,
and father stood up
with us for the rapid legality
we followed with lobster
and champagne at the Gandy Dancer.
Depressed the next
morning, I *knew* it was a mistake. I was
wrong. We remarried
five years later in New Hampshire, joyful
in a wooden church,
a Saturday afternoon in April,
only Jack Jensen our
friend and minister with us, saying
the prayer book's words
among lilies and wine in holy shadow.

❦

It didn't matter that
I had toasted the Queen at Oxford
        while Jane crayoned
into her *Coronation Coloring Book.*
        Married in the spring,
we flew to London in September, ate
        pub lunches, visited
friends in Cambridge, and found a Maltese
        restaurant in Kensington.
We learned how to love each other
        by loving together
good things wholly outside each other.
        We took the advice of my
dear depressed and heartsick Aunt Liz,
        who wrote us at our flat
in Bloomsbury: "Have fun while you can."

                    ✿

        My friend Bill Grabb owned
a one-man hot-air balloon, and matched me
        with a balloonist friend
whose wicker gondola carried two.
        The ascension was set
for six A.M., Barton Hills Country
        Club. I wore black tie
as we slid thirty miles an hour. Propane
        hissed while we rose, but when
we turned it off at three hundred feet
        or a thousand, silence
plaited its transparent gondola

around the gondola.
Cows lurched in circles, and Michigan
farmers ran inside to fetch
their wives. We waved for half an hour
and dragged to a crash
landing in a field of beans, packing up
and paying damages.
Jane drove us back in the Chevrolet
that zagged to follow
our jaunt, approximately as nervy
as the high, volatile,
untethered free flight of new marriage.

❀

At spring training —
forty-four years old, two hundred and fifty
pounds, with a full beard
and hair hanging to my shoulders — I tried
out for the Pittsburgh
Pirates. For seven days I ran bases,
did infield, and took
BP while the real ballplayers heehawed.
My body turned red, swole,
and stiffened. At the end of the week
it took me an hour
to get out of bed. Jane observed my play
from the stands — larky,
amused, but worried about heart attacks —
and heard a grandfather
explain to a puzzled eight-year-old

with outfielder's glove
and scorecard that I was some old catcher.

❀

The first three years
of our marriage, we picnicked with Benjamin
        and Edward: Beaujolais
Villages, Brie, pâté, and sourdough bread
        on the soft grass.
We took pleasure in these friends from Toronto
        who loved food and literature
as we waited for Shakespeare,
        Shaw, or Chekhov
at eight o'clock in Stratford, Ontario.
        The plays were rapture,
better our companionship in gossip,
        theater, and poetry;
in goose liver, grapey wine, and cheese.
        When Edward and Benjy
split up, we had moved to Eagle Pond.
        We missed them, Stratford,
and picnics; we settled down to Kearsarge,
        red flannel hash,
pond summers, radio baseball, each other.

❀

We lived on our own
in the long white farmhouse where as a child
        I daydreamed to live. Leaves

changed and fell; we stacked six cords of wood.
　　　Jane painted our names
on the outsized mailbox. The first Sunday
　　　I thought they'd expect us
to go to church, and we heard the young
　　　preacher quote "Rilke,
the German poet." Weeks later, when Jane
　　　had the flu on a Sunday
and would stay home, I felt restless.
　　　At the last minute I cried,
"I can't stand it," and rushed to church.

✿

　　　When it dropped to
thirty below, we kept four woodstoves burning:
　　　the kitchen cooking range,
the parlor Glenwood, the new Jøtul,
　　　and in Jane's study
the dateless old tin and iron stove we found
　　　in the back chamber.
Before bed I lugged seven tilting loads
　　　from the woodshed, filled up
the Glenwood and closed it for the night.
　　　At five in the morning
I opened its doors — shaking ash down,
　　　exposing gold coals —
to load it again, and went back to bed
　　　while outraged maple warmed
the house. Sitting to work, I would sense
　　　that a stove was needy
and get up to stretch and haul some wood.

85

The Old Life

✿

We walked in the white house
like ghosts among ghosts who cherished us.
Everything we looked at
exalted and raptured our spirits: —
full moon, pale blue
asters, swamp maples Chinese red, ghost birches,
stone walls, cellar holes,
and lopsided stretched farmhouses like ours.
The old tenants watched us
settle in, five years, and then the house
shifted on its two-hundred-
year-old sills, and became our house.

✿

Our first summers here
we spent our afternoons at Eagle Pond,
walking down to it
after lunch with our books. Water lilies
floated in Bullfrog Cove;
birch trees tilted from the curving shore
where we lopped weeds
to carve a recess among wild strawberries
and moss that sprouted
tiny red flowers under white pines and oak.
Jane lay in the sun.
Reading and dozing I sat in the shade.
We swam, dried off,
and swam again, to the music of young girls

86

squealing as they water-skied
from the camp on the pond's west shore.

One year the pond turned
orange and stank, seepage from money's dump,
 and we stopped visiting
Eagle Pond on summer afternoons,
 one subtraction among
the days that give, take away, give, take.

✿

Jane had published only
her first book. After my friend Robert
 and I had concluded
our poetry reading, the English
 professor, learning
that Jane Kenyon was also a poet,
 was flabbergasted
and aghast. "Don't you feel dwarfed?" he asked her.

✿

The first snow every
year delivered me into a half-light
 of pleasurable
lassitude and waking dream, a hazy
 eerie contentedness
where poems blossomed from cold whiteness.
 For Jane the first haying
brought another transport, as new green

                    grass tumbled over bright
        blades into swaths, and the fishbone fields
                    dried in the long sun
        for our farmer neighbor to flip over,
                    rake, bale, and truck off,
        to feed his animals with all winter.
                    Jane gazed at our fields
        from the front porch, loony and ecstatic,
                    as she hung out wash
        on the clothesline using wooden clothespins.

                                    ✣

                    In the bliss of routine
        — coffee, love, pond afternoons, poems —
                    we feel we will live
        forever, until we know we feel it.

                                    ✣

                    In June the Fair Committee
        apportioned labor, choosing Ruth
                    for White Elephants because
        "she's ninety and can't do too much."
                    Mary Jane did Fancywork;
        the Home-Made Ice Cream concession
                    belonged to Audrey
        and the Bouleys. The Supper Committee
                    worked longest and hardest.
        Jane baked eleven loaves of French bread
                    for the Food Table —

and seven casseroles and one peach pie
      for Supper. Afterward,
we set up for the Auction. Forrest
      or Bill or Doug or I
hawked everybody's junk back and forth:
      ruinous Pennzoil
caps, bent bicycles, chairs without rungs, black-
      and-white TVs lacking
plugs, bottles, coffee mugs, and ice skates.
      Sometimes strangers pulled up
to watch as we performed the Auction
      on the small hillside
beside the church. Delivering debris
      for dimes, once I changed
a hundred-dollar bill. Massachusetts.

             ❁

Curled on the sofa
in the fetal position, Jane wept day
      and night, night and day.
I could not touch her; I could do nothing.
      Melancholia fell
like the rain over Ireland for weeks
      without end.
             I never
belittled her sorrows or joshed at
      her dreads and miseries.
How admirable I found myself.

             ❁

Jane spent a morning
picking dandelion greens with Mabelle,
    our ninety-year-old cousin,
then stewed the greens up with salt pork
    according to practice,
as she made red flannel hash out of
    leftover boiled dinner,
grinding up beets to make the redness
    according to practice.
This was the place where we chose to live.
    Unlike Mabelle, or Kate
and Wesley, we flew to New Orleans
    and London, to Shanghai
and Calcutta, reading our poems.
    We smiled without stopping
at receptions in South Dakota
    and Ohio. We bowed
to applause, submitted to questions
    about how we got
ideas, slept flying home contented,
    and deposited
checks, according to another practice.

                    ✿

Forty years ago this
spring Robin and I made the journey
    from Oxford to Charterhouse
on a bright day, changing trains twice,
    talking continually
as we strolled the paradisal

sward of his school
among daffodils in an English April.
    Last October I saw him
at the London Clinic: confused,
    skeletal, panicked,
and confident of recovery. In
    November Monica
scattered his ashes from a dinghy
    into the Channel.
That day in nineteen fifty-two we rode
    back to the college
in a van of House cricketers who stopped
    for pints of bitter
at every pub. Robin and I were tired,
    but talked as men in their
twenties talk about what they will do,
    friends now and always,
or until we died, if that could happen.

✿

    If I press Play instead
of Record, and howl that the machine
    has busted, or if I plug
the two ends of one extension
    cord triumphantly
together, or if I discard the fresh
    milk and drink the sour
without noticing there is a difference,
    I am addressed with
affection as Old Seven and a Half.

Jane and Philippa
recall the time a university
telephoned for
my hat size; I didn't have an idea.
The helpful caller
suggested, "Maybe seven and a half?"
I was overheard to ask,
"Would that be the circumference?"

✿

Scott Nearing was ninety-five
when he lectured at Holderness.
Bent almost double,
smiling, he scuttled to the prep school's stage.
"The world's population
doubles every thirty-five years. Rome
had its day; now we've
had ours. I come from Victoria's time
when England's ships owned the seas —
and pound sterling everything else.
Our civilization's done for."
His face crazed with wrinkles broke
and re-formed as he laughed.
"After Rome went down," he said, "there were
a thousand years when nothing
happened."
The speaker who followed,
a new-age Jungian
analyst, shared cheerful news with us:
"Systems analysis,"
he declared, "will replace linear

thinking as we
enter an era of noncompetitive
    sports, visual
literacy, and nonjudgmentality."

                    ✿

        To celebrate her
eighteenth birthday, we took my mother
        to Bermuda, persuading her
in spite of her arthritis.
        (She couldn't decide,
then one day confessed on the telephone
        that she had bought a dress.)
We drove two hours to La Guardia,
        borrowed a wheelchair,
flew on Delta, and bused to the hotel.
        She loved the fresh melons,
the baked fish, and before dinner one
        rum punch slowly cherished.
The day before we left, we wandered
        by taxi for two hours
past pastel stucco houses, past stacked
        graveyards, past roses
in a saturation of perfumed air.
        Mostly, for four days,
she lay on her bed by the balcony,
        her windows open to wind
that smelt like Evening in Paris
        and ruffled her new dress
as it hung green and gold on a hook.

✿

Seven weeks away
from the New Hampshire desk, on the last day
of our trip, in Sapporo,
we ate noodle soup with the head
of the Hokkaido
Historical Museum. In his good
English, and with
embarrassment, the director desired us
to check the grammar
and diction of a photograph's caption
he had composed in English —
and his two sentences lacked one
"the." But I also noticed
that if he reversed the order
of clauses, the first
sentence would gain energy; the second,
turned into a dependent
clause, would compress the whole to half
the words and make a witty
shape. My pencil made loops, circling
new orders of diction
and style, my heart pounding with passion.

✿

At Shanghai, poplars
posed by the roadside in the attitudes

of dancers. We promenaded
the Bund observing colors
of a hundred merchant
navies on the sterns of freighters, junks,
tankers, container
carriers — keels of the ten thousand years.

At Beijing, the Gobi's
dust swirled in the Forbidden City.
At Xi'an, a terra-cotta
army marched without motion.
At the Guangzhou hotel,
bellboys and maids wore Groucho Marx masks —
big noses, black glasses —
and collapsed exhausted with laughter.

All night in the soft
sleeper from Xi'an to Chengdu, twisting
huddled in our sweaters
with knapsacks for pillows, we slept to
the locomotive's whistle
and the rapping of iron on iron.
At dawn we watched fields
extend rape's yellow to the horizon.

In the Chengdu hotel,
a fair-sized rat: Jane chased him (I stayed
asleep) into the bathroom
and closed the door. She alerted
the front desk — which was aghast —
and woke me to change rooms. At dawn

we found the rejected rat
drowned in the toilet and despair.

In Shenyang we took
a room in the Liaoning Hotel, old
    and fancy-decrepit,
opposite the town center with its
    huge cement Mao webbed in
by trolleys, their rails and their wires.
    At night we walked past
brightly lit noodle shops loud with young men.

At dawn the Mongolian
square turned green with quilted figures
    doing tai chi. At nine
P.M., in the hotel's ballroom, a
    dance band played swing
music under a revolving sequined ball
    where young Shenyang attended
to the fox trot, Charleston, and waltz.

Meeting us at the airport,
the professor of English and
    the vice chancellor bowed
from their waists to greet the distinguished
    Ampart poets. Within one hour
we were hugging each other,
    telling jokes and stories, slapping
our thighs, dear friends forever.

I remember: new
hotels elevating among hovels;

a tractor abandoned
at the edge of a field of barley
    where a single man pulled
a wooden plow; wind harsh at the Wall;
    an old dog on her morning
walk, halting to gaze at our train.

❈

    My whole life of writing,
I've made home movies of Wesley Wells
    telling stories,
laughing, and teasing. He recited poems
    in the tie-up, orated
about President Franklin D.
    Roosevelt, and died
at seventy-seven. I see him still —
    his cheekbones, his sayings,
his gait — as if he lived in this house.
    When I die he dies
unless he endures in the affection
    and accent I daily
attribute to my grandfather's voice.

❈

    I walked from the yard
into the kitchen of my mother's house
    on a hot morning, hearing
footsteps approach from the sunporch
    through the parlor
in a familiar cadence. When the person

entered the kitchen,
it was someone who looked like me, just like
me. I gazed into this face
that stared back, puzzled or annoyed,
me but not me: I who was
thinking, or who write these lines now,
lived inside a body
that felt its feet touch linoleum,
that heard its own heart
beating in panic, not the other's heart.
When we stepped closer,
we held each other fast by the elbows.

✿

As we drove down
Route 91 toward Yale–New Haven
                              (she lay
in the cardiac unit
of intensive care, substantial
and breathing, but I couldn't
look into her seamed livid face
without flicking my eyes
to the monitor above her head
which marked her heart's weary,
stable, ragged beating)
                              I daydreamed
that my mother, entering
Heaven, met my father again.
The bent-over white-
haired woman of eighty embraced a man

dead thirty years, upright,
with black hair and an unwrinkled face.

&

First Emily was born
with red hair in New York, and four days
later Allison emerged
in New Hampshire with *her* red hair.
I bought a Polaroid.
One-Hour Finishing took a whole hour.
Over the next six years
I watched character temper and fix,
as they became who
they are and will be. I rolled on the floor
mooing, crowing, bah-bahing,
and embraced their small blond sisters —
Arianna, Abigail —
and Peter the brother-cousin,
with *his* red hair.
My old poem claimed that I wanted to live
here, somebody's
grandfather. Today I show two six-year-olds
sheep's wool in the attic
Sheared from B. C. Keneston's First sheep
on the old Farm   Carded
at Otterville   eighteen-Forty-eight

&

When my parents
celebrated or relaxed, it was always
by going out to dinner.

When my father died, my mother
　　kept eating out with friends,
with neighbors, and, in the years when she
　　substitute-taught, with
other teachers. Then her friends died. For ten
　　years arthritis kept her
mostly stiff in her Barcalounger,
　　watching birds and school-
children, squirrels and dogs. Turning ninety,
　　she stayed in the sunroom
not too far from toilet and kitchen.
　　She cooked in five-minute
episodes of standing up. One day
　　I heard her mention —
with the scorn we keep for other people's
　　frivolities, like
Learjets or gilded toenails — "Oh, I don't
　　want to go out." She sewed
aprons and made scrubbers from nylon
　　net. She reread Agatha
Christie in large-type editions.

☆

　　Fifteen years ago his heart
infarcted and he stopped smoking.
　　At eighty he trembled
like a birch but remained vigorous
　　and acute.
　　　　　　When they married
fifty years ago, I was twelve.

I observed the white lace
veil, the mumbling preacher, and the flowers
          of parlor silence
and ordinary absurdity; but
          I thought I stood outside
the parlor.
                    For two years she dwindled
          by small strokes
into a mannequin — speechless almost, almost
          unmoving, eyes open
and blinking, fitful in perception —
          but a mannequin that suffered
shame when it stained the bedsheet.
          Slowly, shaking with purpose,
he carried her to the bathroom,
          undressed and washed her,
dressed her in clean clothes, and carried her back
          to CNN and bed. "All
you need is love," sang John and Paul:
          He touched her shoulder; her eyes
caressed him like a bride's bold eyes.

                    ✿

Walking with Gus
on New Canada Road in January —
          among hemlocks black against
profound snow, among stands of birch
          like tall thin upright
columns of snow — I stopped to watch a wild
          turkey crossing the narrow

gravel road heading upmountain,
            his grotesque old-man's head
jerking back and forth in the manner
            of turkeys. Gus turned
his head to see what I stared at, and stood
            stock still, pointing attentive
to the black-feathered gait and hurl,
            the uncanny shambling
feathery brute figure of old woods.

                              ✿

            Gussie treed a bear cub
on his morning walk with Jane. In mist
            on a July Fourth morning,
a moose clattered on the blacktop
            as I drove for the *Globe*.
When I walked by the pond in the white
            waste of February
a great black otter stretched itself out
            on thin ice near running
water. Last night at Piero and
            Julia's La Meridiana,
our waitress paused and gestured
            out the window
at the field where a young coyote emerged
            from pine to taste the late
August air, sniffed, padded cautiously
            for five minutes, then
returned to shadow — as diners returned
            from the window to their
Bordeaux and pink standing racks of lamb.

✿

My old Connecticut
friend — novelist, runner-up each year
for the Nobel, each year
beaten out by "some pinko hacker" —
drove up for the day
from Hartford with his new daughter and young
wife. We met each other
in our twenties — fresh lords of the word,
secure in foreknowledge
of permanent alienation,
working each in his cell
of ambitious poverty and rage
for fame. We were brilliant,
proud, shrewd, and stupid as we blundered
through divorce, shame, prizes,
and remarriage. . . into the amends
and agues of age.
                              He sat
sighing, looking through indexes
of literary
biographies to revisit insults
dead writers paid him.
He adored his infant daughter and wife.
"Isn't she beautiful?"
he said, indifferently, of both
or either. Then he closed
his eyes, leaned back on the sofa, sighed
deeply, and murmured:
"Tell me a story, how it used to be."

The Old Life

Jane's father played
le jazz hot in Paris and on the Lido,
        teenage piano player
in the nineteen twenties, rolling
        his barrelhouse left hand
three years for Lud Gluskin et son Jazz.
        In nineteen thirty,
he jammed with Bix Beiderbecke at Walled Lake,
        then played with itinerant
dance bands like Goldkette's, a decade
        of suitcases and hotels.
Jane thought that her father Reuel
        was exactly like
anybody's father, and her mother
        like anybody's mother,
who sang with swing bands in nightclubs,
        then played cocktail
piano singing in Chicago barrooms.
        Last year Polly found
publicity shots of inscrutable
        nineteen thirty-four
glamour. When I inquired, "What did your first
        husband do?" my small
soft-spoken mother-in-law, eighty-one,
        answered me cheerfully:
"He was a professional gambler."

✿

At three, living in the rented
house on Winette Street, I strayed
        three blocks away, and the word
lost crashed in my ears like the sea,
        until a neighbor
led me back to my house and my mother.
        When Dr. Clark telephoned
about the hourglass-shaped lesion
        in my liver, I was sixty-
three and lost. Jane and I lay
        on the painted bed
weeping and hugging. Only the body
        of the other — rocking,
hopeless, wet-faced — provided us house.

✿

Just before I entered
Dartmouth-Hitchcock for the procedure,
        Jane met the lawyer Buckwell
at the store, who routinely asked
        how we were doing.
When she told him, Bucks looked melancholy:
        "Gosh. I never did get
to know Don, the way I wanted to."

✿

The three-year-old with tight
yellow curls stood by the back porch's
        screen door, his stolid legs

in shorts, wearing a sweater, holding
     a carrot in his right
hand: I feel myself inside his face.
     For a week my mother
pulled a carrot from the back garden
     for supper; tonight
I pulled it myself, bringing it to her.
     Her pride wrote penny postcards:
"You'll never guess what Donnie did!"
     Today, sixty years later,
I gaze at the loose flesh of my
     upper arm, where muscle
flourished, sagging wrinkled and puckered
     like the flesh of my calves
and thighs hanging punky and useless.
     As I wait outside
the infusion room for the 5FU
     to heat my hand
with its eighteen cc's of poison, among
     other skeletons
of flesh consuming similar poisons,
     I feel pity for
my wretched body that sickens itself
     to try to remain
itself. Then I disable self-pity
     by the only turn
that reduces it: Among the reading
     in the waiting room,
I observe a copy of *Goodnight Moon*.

✿

Peonies as big as turkeys
protect in each blossom a
        freckle of red, like paint
flecked from a toothbrush — reticent, bold,
        wholly delicate
clumsiness — that softens and elevates
        early bright days
of summer. Late in August a hummingbird
        poises at a peach hollyhock
eight feet tall, its faint-edged pale
        house of flower, and hesitates
to enter the crinks of pink zone.

❀

My best friend wrote
a best seller. (He didn't mean to; it just
        happened.) I remember
the day I realized what all these
        television interviews
and newspaper notices meant
        for money, and called him up,
exclaiming, "You're rich!" My best friend
        defended himself:
"Maybe, but I'm not saving anything!"

❀

In her living room
we gathered my mother's necessary
        or cherished objects

for taking north to the facility
        and care of nurses:
caftans and slippers; magnifying glass;
        checkbook and records;
pretty teacups and Dalton figurines;
        a photograph of my father
at college, grinning sideways
        into the camera
seventy years ago. Tonight she
        slept breathing oxygen
at Yale–New Haven, waking to fret
        over tomorrow's
ambulance ride of four sedated hours
        north from the corner house
we moved to when she was thirty-two
        and I was seven.
                        I paced outside
the Ardmore Street house in
        darkness, on grass
where I tossed a football with my young father
        back and forth, Sunday afternoons,
third grade to fourth, fourth to fifth,
        as if things never ended.
Here is the window well in which
        I kept the turtles I caught
at Johnson's Pond, later finding
        empty shells. The radio
stood by the living room window
        so that I heard the good news
flash from the Philco: A Navy
        patrol plane had spotted

Amelia Earhart's Lockheed intact
    on a Pacific atoll
near Wake Island, and she was safe.

✢

    Katherine wore her hat
as she sat in the lobby whistling
    and calling for her brother, "Byron . . . ?
Byron . . . ?" and dressed to go.
    Barbara, who was bald,
smiled gaily although her mouth pended
    to the left of her nose.
Bob, Mary Jane, Sally, and Edna
    snored in wheelchairs — humped,
contorted, open-mouthed —
        while Benjamin
    and Joan the nurses;
and Lucinda who helped with supper trays,
    mopping, jugs,
and bedpans; and Herbert the respiratory
    technician soothed, calmed, touched,
and caressed
        that one with no face, or
    this one with extra faces,
that one whose prosthesis slipped off,
    or this one who giggled,
or that one who howled like a chained dog,
    or Kathy who politely
inquired if I might be Byron.

＊

Usually I parked
my car by six and opening time
to pick up the *Globe*
at the Kearsarge Mini-Mart, where Amy
made coffee for the seven
regulars in beards, Mobil caps,
jeans, and boots who stood around
for an hour each morning. Looking
solemn, they teased back and forth,
joking about deer and cordwood,
ice-storms and carburetors.
Most days, Amy braided long blond
hair into a tidy coil,
but once a week she wore it loose,
flowing, long enough
to sit on, although Amy never sat.
When I praised her hair, she said,
with a contained smile, "Guys like it."

＊

On Thanksgiving morning
my friend Bill Hancock the carpenter
arrived at Amy's place
at ten to six, carrying cardboard
with a clipping pasted
on it, and Amy dropped everything
to print out carefully
with her lavender Magic Marker:

LOCAL WRITERS ON TV
TONIGHT. DON HALL AND JANE KENYON.

※

When Jane and I married,
nobody in Ann Arbor gave us
        eighteen months. Today
we survived twenty-one years. We made love
        to celebrate, and drove
forty miles to a good restaurant
        to please ourselves with
oil and garlic, mushrooms and blanc de blancs.
        We gazed at each other
over candles with deliberate
        gratitude. A year ago
we feasted in silence, brooding,
        unable not to dwell
upon the operation next week
        to remove half
my liver. It was impossible, dreading
        death, to take pleasure
in the conclusion of twenty good years.

※

In nineteen ninety-three
I was up for the NBA in
        poetry. From the first
day, when I reckoned up the judges
        and nominees, I claimed

The Old Life

A. R. Ammons would win the award.
      Nevertheless, he won it.
When Archie walked past our table
      toward the stage, I reached
for his hand and shook it like a good sport.
      At the reception, the judges
touched my shoulder, dropped their eyes,
      and said my stuff
was terrific. I went to sleep easily,
      mildly let down, and woke
at three-thirty in murderous rage.

      Three hours later, sleeping
for twenty minutes on the shuttle,
      I reasoned with myself:
"Why should anyone win some contest?
      Who, for instance?
When did winning an award mean you were *good?*
      The Pulitzer Prize?
Don't be an ass. The fox is sensible.
      Grow up. Go home. Take a shower.
Sit at your desk, and, as the kids
      at prep school liked
to tell you, 'Go write a poem about it.'"

         ✿

      At sixty-five, on a cool
Thanksgiving morning, I prepared
      dressing for the bird,
my one contribution, and baby-proofed

the house against Peter,
eighteen months old and the fifth grandchild.
    At twelve o'clock noon
he arrived with his sisters, his mother
    and father in a glorious
clutter of cries and snowsuits.
    Then my son Andrew and I
slumped at the television set
    to watch pro football
like all male American upholders
    of family values: turkey
with stuffing, potatoes, rolls,
    squash, turnip, onion, ruptured
spleens, paraplegia, and mince pie.
    With my son I watched
Chicago beat Detroit in Detroit, and
    remembered frigid Tiger
Stadium twenty-five years back,
    when we spent calculated
hours together during years of
    divorce, separation,
the shakes, nausea, and howling loss.

                    ✣

    When Newberry's closed
in Franklin, New Hampshire — homely lime front
    on Main Street, among the closed
storefronts of this mill town depressed
    since nineteen twenty-nine;
with its lunch counter for beans and franks

and coleslaw; with its
bins of peanuts, counters of acrylic,
        hair nets, underwear, workshirts,
marbled notebooks, Bic pens, plastic
        toys, and cheap sneakers;
where Marjorie worked ten years at the iron
        cash register, Alcibide
Monbouquet pushed a broom at night,
        and Mr. Smith managed —
we learned that a man from Beverly
        Hills owned it, who never saw
the streets of Franklin, New Hampshire,
        and drew with a well-groomed hand
a line through "Franklin, New Hampshire."

                    ✿

        In May, nineteen ninety-three,
Tree Swenson and Liam Rector
        married in our back
garden. Liam's daughter Virginia
        carried flowers, and Tree's best friend
Anne from Port Townsend stood with us
        as we spoke "Little Gidding,"
then hurried inside from a storm
        to conclude in the parlor.
That night, we toasted each other
        at Piero's, ate osso
bucco, and photographed ourselves.
        The next day, in ordinary
blue sunlight, Liam and Tree

drove off toward Boston
to take up head colds, movies, the mortgage,
 AA, depression, love, skin
cancer, poems, debt, and rapture.

 ✿

 Forty years ago,
in my twenties, with a son and a new
 job, I worked
on my poems in Ann Arbor at six A.M.
 When Andrew came downstairs
to play, in his blue Dr. Denton's,
 with his red hair
and cheerful mien, I wrote him a poem on
 a subject of his choosing —
"Toast," "Milk," "Blueberry Jam," "Cookies";
 he must have been hungry —
which he carried back upstairs, content,
 allowing me silence
and solitude.
 Each morning to get
 started I improvised
blank verse, a version of the fable
 of the Disguised King
and the Imperious Host. After six
 months of using it
for warm-ups, I arrived at an ending
 and put the poem
away. Later, I no longer aspired
 to black coffee,

clarity, and the lucid sensible Muse
    of quarterly stanzas.
The Muse of Unconsciousness declared
    Buicks that sang the hedgehog's
noon.
        It follows that, at sixty-
five — living in New Hampshire
without teaching, with Jane Kenyon,
    attempting to put
death off, enjoying without stint the five
    dear children of my children,
working in wonted frustration
    and absorbedness —
I found the old fable, word-processed it,
    and each day revise it
in renewed bliss of iambic feet,
    inversions, enjambment,
and caesurae. I count up to five
    three thousand times
to invent a king who invited himself
    to his own castle
and mortified impulse by rectitude.

        ✿

    Four weeks of India:
temples, lilies, conversation, heat,
    and instruction. When
we entered P. Lal's parlor for biscuits
    and tea, Sanskrit
poems and literary discussion, he

announced our topic,
asking, "What do you think of irony?"

In the market seventy
stalls of fruit sellers piled apples,
pears, pomegranates,
kiwis, and pineapples in pyramids
as carefully constructed
as the Taj, or the arrangements
of carrots, cabbages,
leeks, and peppers in vegetable stalls.

Friends invited us
to the Club, clearly something established
and left behind by the Raj,
with its eighteen bright green fairways
in downtown Calcutta. We sipped
Black & White Scotch for two hours,
then dined under grand
chandeliers, without drinking the water.

The odor of flowers
in the market — overwhelming jasmine,
red roses, marigolds,
tuberoses, and lotus blossoms —
mixed with another,
as we crossed to the sidewalk shoemaker's:
divers excrements
of camel, dog, elephant, human, cow.

The Old Life

We drove for six hours
from Madras to Pondicherry, on roads
    and tracks through villages
of twenty thousand, past small paddies,
    over wheat spread on the road
for tire thrashing, past water holes
    where women washed
and spread resplendent saris under the sun.

          ✿

    December twenty-first
we assembled at the church festooned
    red and green, the tree
flashing green-red lights beside the altar.
    After the children of Sunday
school recited Scripture, sang,
    and scraped out solos,
they retired to dress for the finale,
    to perform the pageant
again: Mary and Joseph kneeling
    cradleside, Three Kings,
shepherds and shepherdesses. Their garments
    were bathrobes with moth holes,
cut down from the church's ancestors.
    Standing short and long,
they stared in all directions for mothers,
    sisters and brothers,
giggling and waving in recognition.
    Then at the South
Danbury Church, a moment before Santa

arrived with her ho-hos
and bags of popcorn, in the half-dark
of whole silence, God
entered the world as a newborn again.

✿

At ninety, bed-bound
in the facility, my mother gasped
as she sucked oxygen
through cannulae. Shyly she confessed
her tormenting obsession
to eat a piece of apple pie.
We watched her chew
the slice from Letha's Family Restaurant,
smiling as she paused
to breathe, her face gorgeous with happiness.

✿

I sat at her bedside
every afternoon for half an hour,
dwelling in the luminous
air of her pride and affection.
She died quietly
and quickly on a morning in late March
before I could reach her,
while a tender woman held her hand.
I sat with her white body
half an hour and kissed her forehead,
and at night the telephone
rang although no one was calling.

The Old Life

＊

Insofar as coffins
can be pretty, it was a pretty
coffin I picked out
for my mother. Just twenty years ago
my mother Lucy picked out
a coffin for her mother Kate.
Did they still carry
that model? It was stored in the garage,
fiberboard covered with gray
fabric, cheapest box at Chadwick's.
I chose the Vermont Hardwood,
dark and shiny. At calling hours,
we said that her mouth
was wrong. It was a comfort, I suppose.

＊

She lay in the coffin,
her hands arranged so that the jewels
of her rings gleamed
in the spot shining from the ceiling: diamond
engagement ring and sapphire
— *star* sapphire, she always called it —
that my father gave her.
Charlie Hafner in his pinstriped suit
told me that we bury women
with their wedding bands only.
I could not watch him
return to the coffin to fetch the rings.

The engagement diamond
went to my son, his wife and daughters.
When my daughter had praised
the sapphire, it pleased my mother. Now
Philippa wears the *star*
sapphire. To please me? It pleases me.

✿

The old woman's tiny watch,
"twenty-four jewels," went into
Jane's jewelry box,
unlikely to be wound again. Lucy
wore it for years after
it stopped working, turning it over
to read the engraving
on the back. *Don to Lucy,* it said,
December 1955,
and didn't mention Christmas.
He understood what
would happen by Christmas. Fifty-two on
the sixth, he died
the twenty-second. Interred on Christmas Eve.

✿

A decade ago, when
Philippa married Gerry, I slipped
and spoke of the wedding
as a funeral. Then yesterday,
as we drove home

from my mother's interment, I sighed deeply,
saying to Jane, "It's good;
it's *good* that I married my mother."

✿

I woke to a bluish
mounded softness where the Honda was.
I broomed off the windshield
and drove to the Kearsarge Mini-Mart
before Amy opened
to yank my *Globe* out of the bundle.
Back, I set a cup
of coffee beside Jane, still half-asleep,
murmuring stuporous
thanks in the aquamarine morning.
Then I sat in my blue chair
with blueberry bagels and strong
black coffee reading news,
the obits, the comics, and the sports.
Carrying my cup
twenty feet, I sat myself at the desk
for this day's engagement
with the revisions of a whole life.

✿

Blueberry bagels
and the *Globe*. We walked in our daily fields
ignorant of the moment
but knowing that grass would collapse

one day into oblivion.
Every three months a Hitchcock
    tech drew a titre
of my blood; a week later the phone rang
    with numbers to water
the green meadow or burn it away.
    Together we worried
over my days remaining until
    on a Monday Jane's
nose bled. By bedtime, oxymoronic
    poison dripped murderous
reprieve into her blood's white water.

    ✿

Back at the motel, after
all day by her bed, I walked up
    and down, talking
to myself without making a sound, staying
    clear, and made a slip
of the tongue: "My life has leukemia."

WITHOUT

we live in a small island stone nation
without color under gray clouds and wind
distant the unlimited ocean acute
lymphoblastic leukemia without seagulls
or palm trees without vegetation
or animal life only barnacles and lead
colored moss that darkens when months do

hours days weeks months weeks days hours
the year endures without punctuation
february without ice winter sleet
snow melts and recovers but nothing
without thaw although cold streams hurtle
no snowdrop or crocus rises no yellow
no bright leaves of maple without autumn

no spring no summer no autumn no winter
no rain no peony thunder no woodthrush
the book is a thousand pages without commas
without mice maple leaves windstorms

no castles no plazas no flags no parrots
without carnival or the procession of relics
intolerable without brackets or colons

silence without color sound without smell
without apples without pork to rupture gnash
unpunctuated without churches uninterrupted
no orioles ginger noses no opera no
without fingers daffodils cheekbones
the body is a nation a tribe dug into stone
assaulted white blood broken to fragments

provinces invade bomb shoot shell
strafe execute rape retreat and attack
artillery sniper fire helicopter gunship
grenade burning murder landmine starvation
the ceasefire lasts forty-eight hours
then a shell explodes in a market
pain vomit neuropathy morphine nightmare

confusion terror the rack the screw
vincristine ara-c cytoxan vp-16
loss of memory loss of language losses
foamless unmitigated sea without sea
delirium whipmarks of petechiae pcp
multiple blisters of herpes zoster
and how are you doing today I am doing

one afternoon say the sun comes out
moss takes on greenishness leaves fall
the market opens a loaf of bread a sparrow
a bony dog wanders back sniffing a lath
it might be possible to take up a pencil
unwritten stanzas taken up and touched
beautiful terrible sentences unuttered

the sea unrelenting wave gray the sea
flotsam without islands broken crates
block after block the same house the mall
no cathedral no hobo jungle the same women
and men they long to drink hayfields
without dog or semicolon or village square
without monkey or lily without garlic

Notes

The Night of the Day

It was only six months after the night of stories
that Dave Perkins's back wouldn't quit aching
even when he took time off from loading his truck.
When they opened him up, as Belle explained it,
they let the air in. Paul quit school for the mill
in Penacook and Belle sold up, moving to Lebanon
and her sister's mobile home. When Peg Jones retired,
Ned took over, grinning with new teeth. Sherman
drinks coffee at the Mini-Mart every morning — grayer,
fatter, and gossipy as ever. Yesterday he told me
that Victoria, home from work the afternoon before,
discovered Willy stiff and white in the tie-up.

The Thirteenth Inning

"In *The Museum of Clear Ideas*, Hall invents names for himself
— 'K.C.,' 'William Trout,' 'Horace Horsecollar,' 'Mr. Zero' — to
record his every whimpering change of mood. Annoyingly, he
drops references to his own work as if his readers were scholars
of Donald Hall. In a long poem called 'Baseball,' followed by te-

dious inevitable 'Extra Innings,' Hall explains the game of baseball to the late Kurt Schwitters, Dada collagist: a quaint conceit, a dainty device. Blessedly, Hall's game ends with a home run in the twelfth inning; no fan — of poetry or of baseball — would wish for a thirteenth."

— Adam Roberts, *The Internal Review of Books*

The Old Life

Interviewer: Tell us more about McPoems. What is it you dislike so much?

Hall: Oh, they're boring prosy little anecdotes out of memory, where the poets look back on themselves, often in childhood, with *such* affection and pity, and with a continual, crepuscular melancholy. Sometimes they pretend to mock themselves, but McPoems are perfect in their narcissism — home movies, photographed through linoleum, cut and spliced to flatter the star.

Page 57. PLC: Platoon Leader Corps.
Page 59. JCR: Junior Common Room.
Page 96. Ampart: American Participant, State Department cable
 language.

Without

Unfamiliar words are mostly chemicals infused to initiate or sustain remission from leukemia. Petechiae are red marks on the skin that indicate a deficiency of platelets in the blood; platelets help with clotting. PCP is a form of pneumonia common to people with compromised immune systems, like sufferers from AIDS or ALL (acute lymphoblastic leukemia). Herpes zoster: shingles.